THE *Future of Taiwan*

THE *Future*

M. E. Sharpe INC., WHITE PLAINS, NEW YORK

Edited by Victor H. Li

of Taiwan

A DIFFERENCE OF OPINION

A dialogue among:

Trong R. Chai 蔡同榮

Winberg Chai 翟文伯

Parris Hsu-cheng Chang 張旭成

Pi-chao Chen 陳必照

Tan S. Chen 陳唐山

Samuel C. Chu 朱昌崚

Kuang-huan Fan 范光煥

Cho-yun Hsu 許倬雲

Che-tsao Huang 黃哲操

Thomas W. Huang 黃維辛

Tzu-Min Kao 高資敏

Michael Ying-mao Kau 高英茂

Victor Hao Li 李浩

Hung-Mao Tien 田弘茂

Richard Yang 楊日旭

Compiled with the assistance of the
Stanford Journal of International Studies

Copyright © 1980 by M. E. Sharpe, Inc.
901 North Broadway, White Plains, New York 10603

Published simultaneously as Vol. IX, no. 3-4 of *International Journal of Politics*

Library of Congress Catalog Card Number: 80-50142
International Standard Book Number: 0-87332-173-1

Printed in the United States of America

To Our Parents

Contents

Preface

For years to come, the "Taiwan question" is likely to raise exceedingly difficult—and potentially divisive—political and moral issues for the people of the United States, the People's Republic of China (PRC), and the Republic of China (ROC). Recent developments in both the PRC and the ROC, however, provide some hope that a peaceful resolution of this problem can be found. Both sides seem willing to at least think quietly about a range of realistic future possibilities for Taiwan. The PRC is moving rapidly to cement relations with the United States, Japan, and Western Europe. Conflict over Taiwan will greatly disrupt this process. Developments in Taiwan are less dramatic but no less important. Many persons, both in and out of government, are considering what course to follow as a new generation of leaders takes over.

While the formal and rhetorical positions of the PRC, ROC, and other parties remain quite far apart, there may be much less disagreement about what each actually expects to happen in Taiwan or what outcomes each would find acceptable. For example, it seems unlikely that the ROC can maintain indefinitely its claim to represent all of China, making no adjustments in the distribution of political power between Mainlanders and Taiwanese. Similarly, few people believe that the PRC would or could completely take over Taiwan in the near future. Instead, many foresee an intermediate existence for Taiwan wherein it retains a considerable degree of self-control but may also have, in fact or in name, some direct ties to the Mainland.

In an effort to pursue these issues, five persons—Professors Hungdah Chiu, Samuel Chu, Che-tsao Huang, Ying-mao Kau, and I—organized a conference to discuss the future of Taiwan. We wanted to get beyond rhetoric and polemics and examine the underlying realities of the Taiwan question. Up to now, people holding different views on this issue tended to talk at, rather than with, each other.

In inviting participants, we believed it critically important that all points of view be represented. We sought a balance of persons favoring the PRC, the ROC, the Taiwan independence movement, and other positions. The entire process had to be viewed as fair and not stacked in favor of one position or another. Otherwise, invitees would not participate, and outside observers would ignore the results. We also wanted a significant number of participants to be Taiwanese.

All of the invitees were Chinese-Americans. This group has special knowledge about the Taiwan question, and also a particularly large stake in how it is resolved. Chinese-Americans should play a major role in the formulation of American policy on the future of Taiwan.

Fifteen persons attended the conference which was co-sponsored by The Johnson Foundation and the Center for East Asian Studies of Stanford University, and held on June 8-10, 1979, at Wingspread, the educational conference center of The Johnson Foundation at Racine, Wisconsin. (See appendix 1 for a list of the participants.) Several other persons were invited but were unable to take part because of schedule conflicts; some submitted written statements after reading the conference transcript. (See appendix 2.)

The discussions were lively and candid. The comments of one participant illustrates the character of these conversations:

Vincent: I have established my life in the United States. Even if I could return to China or Taiwan to take up a permanent position, I probably would not do so. I have come to terms with the fact that my children will live in the United States and my grandchildren may be yellow-haired and blue-eyed. Intellectually, I regard myself as an American of Chinese parentage.

But this does not mean that I have abandoned China emotionally. And of course, my professional work continually involves me in Chinese affairs. Like many other Chinese-Americans, I feel very proud when something is accomplished in China. But I also recognize that there have been some serious mistakes as well. The same thing applies to Taiwan. I have close professional and emotional ties to

Taiwan. I sympathize with its position, but I do not always agree with what it does.

I welcome the opportunity to discuss the future of Taiwan in depth. This is a very rare occasion. I happen to be rather jaundiced toward my fellow Chinese; too many of my friends have never leveled with me about their true feelings on this issue. Many of them, either because their parents are living in Taiwan or China or because their cultural tradition calls for keeping quiet when in doubt, have not spoken out.

I have never met half the people here before. If I were to be typically Chinese, I would restrict my introductory remarks to totally innocuous subjects. But I made up my mind that I must speak out. There is, of course, some risk in doing so, even for a person like myself who does not have any close relatives in China or Taiwan. But all of us must speak out if we are to make any contribution to the solution of the Taiwan problem.

I will try not to offend anyone here, but I intend to be very blunt and frank in our conversations. I hope that you will feel equally free to speak your mind.

The discussions at the June conference were taped and transcribed. I edited this material into chapters II-VII. Each participant has reviewed the text to ensure that his remarks have been accurately reproduced. Chapter I provides some background on American policy toward Taiwan. This chapter also spells out my own views so that the reader can adjust for any biases which I may have inadvertently introduced into the editing process.

Some participants preferred not to be directly quoted; yet we all felt that total anonymity would greatly reduce the impact of the discussions on the reader. Consequently, we agreed to list all the participants, but assign a pseudonym to each in the reproduced conversations.

What do we hope to achieve with this conference and volume? Our goal is to improve public understanding of, and governmental deliberations on, the Taiwan question. Gathering the entire range of views into one volume helps readers make their own judgments about the merits of the case. Moreover, engaging advocates of different positions in a common debate highlights the areas of agreement and disagreement. A number of new analytical and moral perspectives also were introduced. We hope that this initial effort will encourage further dialogue on this difficult and complex issue.

We are very grateful to Leslie Paffrath and Rita Goodman of The Johnson Foundation for their generous financial and intellectual support of this venture. Their long standing interest in United States-China relations has been a significant factor in developing better understanding between the two countries.

We also are very grateful to Chinn Ho and Stuart Ho of the Chinn Ho Foundation for their generous and prompt support of this project. Without their assistance many of the participants would not have been able to attend the conference.

I want to thank the members of the *Stanford Journal of International Studies* for their invaluable help in preparing the manuscript for publication, especially Francis Hogan, John Phillips, Peter Staple, Peter Stern, and David Temin who provided editorial assistance in the early stages of this project.

Finally, I want to express my special appreciation to Carroll Rudy for assistance above and beyond the call of duty.

Victor H. Li
Stanford, California
November 12, 1979

I

Taiwan and America's China Policy: An Introduction

Victor H. Li

> *"The Chinese side reaffirmed its position: The Taiwan question is the crucial question obstructing the normalization of relations between China and the United States."*
> Shanghai Communique, 1972

Despite the completion of the formal normalization process between the United States and the People's Republic of China (PRC) on January 1, 1979, the Taiwan question remains unresolved. Yet the status quo cannot last indefinitely. The PRC still wishes to finish the civil war by reuniting Taiwan with China. At the same time, the Republic of China (ROC) must attempt to clarify and solidify its international status, and thereby facilitate trade, travel, and other relations.

Perhaps most important of all, an internal political dynamic appears to be developing in Taiwan which may lead to important changes on that island. The discussions contained in this volume illustrate the sharp differences that informed and reasonable people have over how change will occur and what the ultimate outcome will or should be. But there is little disagreement over the fact that the process of change in Taiwan will be active and even contentious in the coming years. Moreover, this process is something over which

---

1   As is obvious from the discussions reproduced in the following chapters, there is wide disagreement over the past, present, and future of Taiwan. The views presented in this chapter are my own, and are not necessarily supported by the other contributors to this volume.

neither the United States nor the PRC has much control. And, if changes do occur, neither the United States nor the PRC seems well-prepared to respond.

Indeed, for the next five or ten years the effort to resolve the Taiwan question may be the major source of potential friction between the United States and the PRC. For example, for reasons discussed in subsequent chapters, there is some possibility that Taiwan may move toward de jure or de facto independence. One cannot predict the future; but *if* that development occurs, what will be the American response? The answer to this question is not at all clear. Although the concept of self-determination has popular appeal, any support for some form of independence will conflict with the PRC's fundamental "one-China" principle. The United States then may have to make an enormously difficult moral and political choice between support for self-determination and a possible rupture of relations with the PRC.

The American government's attitude toward Taiwan is a curious mixture of great concern and studied indifference. On the one hand, for the past 30 years the United States has had extraordinarily extensive contacts with Taiwan involving security and military matters, trade and investment, cultural exchanges, and personal ties. Considerable care was taken to ensure that normalization would not disrupt economic, cultural, and other relations.

At the same time, the United States has taken actions which seem to indicate ignorance of or callousness toward the effect of these actions on Taiwan. For example, the Shanghai Communique was issued on February 28, 1972, Peking and Taipei time (but February 27 Washington time). On that date 15 years earlier, ROC troops began to put down a riot in Taiwan, killing several thousand Taiwanese in the process.[2] The "February 28 uprising" plays an important role in PRC propaganda against the ROC. The issuance of the communique on the anniversary of that event has a significance for Taiwan—and the PRC—which I believe the United States did not consider.

Another example of the American government's apparent lack of concern for Taiwan's feelings involves Zbigniew Brzezinski's visit to China in May 1979. He entered the PRC on the same day that Chiang Ching-kuo was being inaugurated president in Taiwan. A third

---

2   On the February 28 incident, see George Kerr, Formosa Betrayed (1965).

example is that Chiang Ching-kuo was informed of the U.S. normalization of relations with the PRC by being roused out of bed at 2 a.m.
Moreover, the announcement was made in the middle of an important
national election on Taiwan, and led to its suspension—a consequence which the United States may not have anticipated or desired.

I do not believe the United States took these actions to deliberately hurt Taiwan or to show special support for the PRC. Instead,
they probably occurred because the American government's attention is so directed at the PRC that events on Taiwan are often ignored
or overlooked.

One cause of this problem is that the PRC is much larger and
more important to American strategic concerns. In addition, for the
past 30 years the United States has viewed Taiwan as a passive party,
doing essentially what we told it to do. Sometimes we had to tighten
the reins and at other times we had to offer incentives, but control
and initiative were essentially in our hands. Up until now this
perception of Taiwan was correct. But I do not think it is any longer.
New developments in Taiwan are likely to lead to its initiating, rather
than merely reacting to, change.

A. A Perspective on Taiwan

A major factor in Taiwan's internal politics is that the leadership
of the central government is getting very old. For example, the
members of the Legislature (which is similar to our Congress) and the
National Assembly (which meets periodically to elect the President
and Vice-president) average well over 70 years in age. Obviously,
they will soon be replaced by a new generation of leaders.

These two national bodies possess a second special characteristic
besides elderly membership. More than 90 percent of the members of
the Legislature and more than 95 percent of the National Assembly
were elected in 1947.[3] These persons have not stood for reelection
since that time. After all, a representative from Shanghai could
hardly go back to his district and constituents after 1949.

Incidentally, this circumstance explains in part why it is so
difficult for the Taiwan government to cease claiming to be the
government of all China. Such an adjustment, while fully in accord

---

3   *See generally* Ralph Clough, Island China (1978).

with reality, would remove the basis of legitimacy for many office-holders in the central government.

Consequently, the people on Taiwan, including both the Taiwanese (the term used to describe persons whose ancestors came from China to Taiwan over the past several hundred years) and the Mainlanders (persons coming from China to Taiwan after 1945), vote for only a tiny fraction of these national level bodies. In addition, some Taiwanese are dissatisfied because they constitute 85 percent of the population, yet hold only a small number of important government and party positions.[4]

A combination of factors—the passing of the old generation of leaders, the island's great economic and educational achievements, and growing international scrutiny—have created a political atmosphere in Taiwan conducive to and demanding of change. In addition, so much has changed for Taiwan in the international arena since 1971: expulsion from the United Nations, President Nixon's 1972 visit to the PRC, normalization of PRC-Japanese relations, the death of Chiang Kai-shek, and normalization of PRC-U.S. relations. Domestic changes are now needed to enable Taiwan to meet the challenge of international survival. There has been a growing call for a redistribution of political power to more accurately reflect the realities of the island.[5]

The electoral process illustrates how the internal political dynamic is developing. Taiwan basically has a single party system, consisting of the Nationalist Party (Kuomintang or KMT) and two other very small parties. In the past, running for public office was not an effective means by which persons outside the KMT might attain political power. Several opposition candidates did win occasionally, but the elections were dominated by the KMT.

An important change occurred in the 1977 elections for provincial, county, and municipal offices. A number of young Taiwanese politicians, frustrated by the slowness of their advancement through the party or bureaucracy, decided to run for public office in opposition to the KMT.[6] These candidates gained 38 percent of the popular

---

4   *See* chapters IV and V, *infra.*
5   *See* chapters III and V, *infra.*
6   These persons are usually referred to in Chinese as the *"tang-wai jen-shih,"* or "non-KMT personages," and in English as "the opposition."

vote, an astounding feat in an essentially single party state. There also were riots in Chungli and Kaohsiung over alleged election fraud perpetrated by the Nationalists.[7]

Another election was scheduled to be held on December 23, 1978 for 38 seats (out of approximately 400) in the Legislature and 56 seats (out of approximately 1,200) in the National Assembly. The campaign was lively and aggressive on all sides, but was suspended after the normalization announcement. The effect of the suspension on the internal political developments in Taiwan is still unclear.

What are some of the possibilities? Here, I stress that I am speculating; my intention is to provoke thought rather than predict the future.

At one extreme, conservative elements within the KMT may attempt to crack down on the opposition. Such actions already may be taking place. For example, in April 1979, a military court sentenced Yu Teng-fa, a 76-year-old opposition leader from Kaohsiung, to eight years imprisonment for copying and distributing a "subversive" article from *Asahi Shimbun* and failing to report the activities of an alleged PRC agent.[8] Yu's supporters claim that the trial was an effort to harass and intimidate opposition politicians. Of course, whether this assertion is in fact true or false cannot be readily determined by observers in the United States. Nevertheless, the point is that opponents of the government may use the Yu case as a rallying point for protest, and this in turn may lead the government to impose more restrictions. If the crackdown expands in scope or virulence, the image of "Free China" will erode further, leading to a loss of American public and Congressional support.

Toward the other end of the spectrum of possibilities is a takeover of power, gradual or sudden, by Taiwanese political leaders. These persons clearly desire more control over their own destiny; some may even favor an independent state of Taiwan. But they are sophisticated politicians who know that independence is opposed both by the KMT, in part because its own legitimacy would be undercut, and by the PRC, because such an action would violate the one-China principle. With the exception of the Taiwan independence

---

7   For a detailed description of the election campaign and riot, see Lin Chen-chieh & Chang Fu-chung, Hsuan-chu wan-sui [Long Live Elections] (Taiwan, 1977). This book has been banned in Taiwan.

8   *See* chapter II, *infra*.

movement,[9] Taiwanese politicians have generally avoided the term independence, preferring that Taiwan merely be able to act in an independent manner without making a change in the juridical status of the island.

I am not suggesting that either of these two extreme possibilities will in fact occur. There are other less drastic and more likely scenarios. Rather, my point is that developments are taking place on Taiwan which may substantially change its political relations with the United States and the PRC. We must therefore begin thinking about how to cope with possible future developments on Taiwan. Yet people both in and out of the government are not doing so. Once again, we may be caught unprepared and may be confronted with a situation we just as soon would have avoided.

Moral Obligations

Over 30 years ago, in a world that was very different, the United States provided massive military and other assistance to Taiwan when such assistance was sorely needed. In subsequent years, the United States contributed greatly to the remarkable growth of that island.

At some point, the original American commitments to Taiwan for military protection and economic assistance will have been fulfilled. Taiwan is not the 51st state which must be defended and assisted under any circumstances and for all time. In the course of helping to build a new society on Taiwan, however, I believe the United States has incurred new obligations to give that society an opportunity to survive and grow.

Taiwan is presently going through a transition from being the Republic of China representing all of China to some new and still undefined status. What that new status should be must be decided by the people on Taiwan. They must consider the offers being tendered by the PRC. If they feel these offers to be unsatisfactory, they must seek better terms or search for new solutions. It is time for Taiwan to take its own problems in hand. If it wishes to continue the fiction of

---

9   For details on the Taiwan independence movement, see chapter IV, *infra*.

being all of China, then it has had ample notice that it must stand alone and face the consequences. If it wishes to reunify with the PRC or adopt some other status, then it must begin the process of change.

B. United States Policy Since 1972

For the past several years the policy question has not been *whether* the United States should normalize relations with the PRC. That was an issue of the late 1960s and early 1970s. It was settled when Mr. Kissinger and President Nixon went to China in 1971 and 1972, respectively. Since that time American policy has been quite consistent: Normalization was begun by a conservative Republican president, affirmed by a moderate Republican president, and completed by a Democratic president. Thus, when President Carter made his announcement on December 15, 1978, one might have been surprised by the timing, but certainly not by the fact that normalization finally had come.

I stress the point of no surprise because opponents of normalization in the United States as well as spokesmen for the government on Taiwan are being disingenuous in asserting that the December 15 action marked a shift in American policy resulting in the betrayal of Taiwan. If there was a betrayal of Taiwan—which I do not believe is the case—then it occurred in 1971. If anyone was truly surprised by normalization in 1978, then the surprise was a result of their own blind refusal to face reality. Taiwan had nearly eight years' notice that normalization would occur.

Thus, the question facing the United States after 1972 was not whether to normalize, but rather *when* and *on what terms*. There was not even much disagreement over the general outline of the terms. The United States had to move ahead on normalization of relations with the PRC while, at the same time, preserving Taiwan's security; that is, to normalize without "abandoning" Taiwan.[10]

---

10   *See generally* Victor H. Li & John W. Lewis, *Resolving the China Dilemma: Advancing Normalization, Preserving Security,* International Security, vol. 2, no. 1, p. 11 (Summer 1977).

Relations with Taiwan Largely Unaffected

The United States has essentially achieved this result. One might quarrel with the Administration about the lack of consultation with Congress, the manner in which the negotiations were carried out, or the precise timing of the announcement. Congress also may have pushed the President further on the security issue than he would have liked to go. Nevertheless, the end result is that normalization was carried out without jeopardizing Taiwan's security or economic well-being.

All commercial and cultural ties with Taiwan will continue as before. The Taiwan Relations Act passed by Congress on April 10, 1979 provides that:

> The absence of diplomatic relations or recognition shall not affect the application of the laws of the United States with respect to Taiwan . . . . Whenever the laws of the United States refer or relate to foreign countries, nations, states, governments, or similar entities, such terms shall include and such laws shall apply with respect to Taiwan.[11]

The Act also provides that rights and obligations concerning contracts or property interests, ownership of property, choice of law rules, Taiwan's standing to sue or be sued, and eligibility for export licenses for nuclear materials also remain unchanged. The President is authorized to grant, on a reciprocal basis, such privileges and immunities to personnel of the new "unofficial" instrumentality to be established by Taiwan (the Coordinating Council for North American Affairs) as may be necessary for the performance of its duties. In addition, the legislative history specifically refers to the Arms Export Act, the Export Administration Act, the Export-Import Act, the Foreign Assistance Act of 1961, the Trade Act of 1974, the Foreign Sovereign Immunities Act of 1976, the Agricultural Trade Development and Assistance Act of 1954, and the Federal Reserve Act, explaining that these laws and programs should apply to Taiwan in the same manner as before derecognition.[12]

---

11   Taiwan Relations Act § 4, 22 U.S.C. § 3303 (Supp. III 1979). See appendix 9.
12   S. Rep. No. 7, 96th Cong., 1st Sess. (1979); H.R. Rep. No. 26, 96th Cong., 1st Sess. (1979); H.R. Rep. No. 71, 96th Cong., 1st Sess. (1979).

The effect of the Taiwan Relations Act is thus to remove all statutory and judicially developed disabilities imposed on de facto entities.[13] For purposes of domestic American law, in the commercial and cultural areas Taiwan will be treated in the same manner as de jure recognized states or governments. Relations in these areas should continue without change. Indeed, Taiwan even gained one unexpected commercial advantage from derecognition: In the normal course of events, it would have become ineligible for Overseas Private Investment Corporation (OPIC) insurance in the near future because the island's per capita income will exceed the $1,000 limit. In order not to have this additional economic blow fall at a time of political uncertainty and tension, the Act extended Taiwan's eligibility for OPIC insurance for three years.[14]

With respect to treaties with Taiwan, President Carter declared in a December 30, 1978 memorandum for all departments and agencies:

> Existing international agreements and arrangements in force between the United States and Taiwan shall continue in force and shall be performed and enforced by departments and agencies beginning January 1, 1979, in accordance with their terms.[15]

Similarly, section 4(c) of the Taiwan Relations Act states:

> For all purposes, including actions in any court in the United States, the Congress approves the continuation in force of all treaties and other international agreements, including multilateral conventions, entered into by the United States and the Republic of China prior to January 1, 1979, and in force between them on December 31, 1978, unless and until terminated in accordance with law.

---

13   *See also* Victor H. Li, *The Law of Non-Recognition: The Case of Taiwan,* Nw. J. Int'l L. & Bus., vol. 1, p. 134 (1979). For a detailed discussion of these disabilities, see Victor H. Li, De-Recognizing Taiwan: The Legal Problems (1977).

14   Taiwan Relations Act § 5, 22 U.S.C. § 3304 (Supp. III 1979); *see also* S. Rep. No. 7, 96th Cong., 1st Sess. 28 (1979).

15   Presidential Memorandum of Dec. 30, 1978, *Relations With the People on Taiwan,* 44 Fed. Reg. 1075 (1979). See appendix 8.

Fifty-nine of the 60 treaties and executive agreements in force as of December 31, 1978 remain unchanged (although many have long had no operational effect).[16]

The sole exception is the Mutual Defense Treaty,[17] which will terminate at the end of 1979.[18] But I believe that the termination of this treaty will not substantially alter the security relations between the United States and Taiwan.

The name "Mutual Defense Treaty" suggests a commitment to come to the defense of Taiwan. But the literal terms of the treaty are more limited. Article 5 states that in the event of an armed attack on Taiwan, the United States "would act to meet the common danger in accordance with its constitutional processes." This clause was designed to allow the United States to have a "second look" before committing American troops. In light of the limitations imposed on the President by the War Powers Resolution and the post-Vietnam public and Congressional attitudes toward American involvement in an Asian war, the American response under article 5 would most likely be limited to making protests and providing arms and other logistical support.

The United States will likely take similar action if an armed attack occurs after the termination of the Mutual Defense Treaty. The unilateral United States statement of December 15, 1978 declares:

> The United States is confident that the people of Taiwan face a peaceful and prosperous future. The United States continues to have an interest in the peaceful resolution of the Taiwan issue and expects that the Taiwan issue will be settled peacefully by the Chinese themselves.[19]

At a White House background briefing for the press the same day, an "Administration Official" was asked:

> Q: Can we continue to sell arms directly to Taiwan during this next year or for any period of time?

---

16   Victor H. Li, De-Recognizing Taiwan, *supra* note 13, at 31-35.
17   Mutual Defense Treaty, Dec. 2, 1954, United States-Taiwan, 6 U.S.T. 433, T.I.A.S. No. 3178.
18   S. Rep. No. 7, 96th Cong., 1st Sess. 17-20 (1979); *see generally* Senate Comm. on Foreign Relations, 95th Cong., 2d Sess., Termination of Treaties: The Constitutional Allocation of Power (Comm. Print 1978).
19   See appendix 5.

Administration Official: I think it is quite clear from the statement that is being made that the United States will continue the full range of commercial relations with Taiwan. As the treaty is being abrogated, we will continue to deliver to Taiwan all the items that have been committed or have been contracted for. And beyond 1979, we will, of course, make our judgments in the light of the prevailing situation, which we hope will be peaceful. But we will, as I said earlier, retain the full range of commerical relations with Taiwan.

Q: Which includes military weapons.

Administration Official: Which includes, if necessary and the situation warrants it, selected defensive weaponry.

. . .

Q: Do we reserve the right to supply military equipment to Taiwan?

Q: We just asked that. He answered.

Administration Official: Let me answer it again so that there is no doubt about that. The treaty will be terminated at the end of 1979. We are giving a one-year notice in accordance with article 10 of the treaty of its termination. After the treaty is terminated at the end of 1979, the United States will give Taiwan access to arms of a defensive character and do so on a restricted basis so as to promote peace and not interfere with peace in that area.

Similarly, Secretary Vance, speaking at a briefing for members of the National Council for U.S.-China Trade and the USA-ROC Economic Council on January 15, 1979, said:

[A]fter the termination of the Mutual Defense Treaty on December 31, 1979, we will continue our previous policy of selling carefully selected defensive weapons to Taiwan. While the PRC said they disapproved of this, they nevertheless moved forward with normalization with full knowledge of our intentions.[20]

---

20   See appendix 7.

Despite Secretary Vance's implication that the PRC will not interfere with continued sale of defensive arms to Taiwan, it should be noted that Chairman Hua's objection to such sales was strongly stated. He was asked at his December 15, 1978 press conference:

Q: Will the U.S. government be permitted to continue providing Taiwan with access to military equipment for defensive purposes?

Hua: Paragraph two of the joint communique which I announced just now states that "[t]he United States of America recognizes the government of the People's Republic of China as the sole legal government of China. Within this context, the people of the United States will maintain cultural, commercial and other unofficial relations with the people of Taiwan." In our discussions on the question of commercial relations, the two sides had differing views. During the negotiations the U.S. side mentioned that after normalization it would continue to sell a limited amount of arms to Taiwan for defense purposes. We made it clear that we absolutely would not agree to this. In all discussions, the Chinese side repeatedly made clear its position on this question. We held that after normalization continued sale of arms to Taiwan by the United States would not conform to the principles of normalization, would be detrimental to the peaceful liberation of Taiwan, and would exercise an unfavorable influence on the peace and stability of the Asia-Pacific region. So our two sides had differences on this point. Nevertheless, we reached an agreement on the joint communique.[21]

The Taiwan Relations act is even more explicit about future U.S.-Taiwan security issues:

Sec. 2(b): It is the policy of the United States:

. . .

(2) to declare that peace and stability in the area are in the political, security and economic interests of the United States, and are matters of international concern;

---

21   See appendix 10.

(3) to make clear that the United States decision to establish diplomatic relations with the People's Republic of China rests upon the expectation that the future of Taiwan will be determined by peaceful means;

(4) to consider any effort to determine the future of Taiwan by other than peaceful means, including by boycotts or embargoes, a threat to the peace and security of the Western Pacific area and of grave concern to the United States;

(5) to provide Taiwan with arms of defensive character; and

(6) to maintain the capacity of the United States to resist any resort to force or other forms of coercion that would jeopardize the security, or the social or economic system, of the people on Taiwan.

. . .

Sec. 3(a): In furtherance of the policy set forth in section 2 of this Act, the United States will make available to Taiwan such defense articles and defense services in such quantity as may be necessary to enable Taiwan to maintain a sufficient self-defense capability.

(b): The President and the Congress shall determine the nature and quantity of such defense articles and services based solely upon their judgment of the needs of Taiwan, in accordance with procedures established by law. Such determination of Taiwan's defense needs shall include review by United States military authorities in connection with recommendations to the President and the Congress.

(c): The President is directed to inform the Congress promptly of any threat to the security or the social or economic system of the people on Taiwan and any danger to the interests of the United States arising therefrom. The President and the Congress shall determine, in accordance with constitutional processes, appropriate action by the United States in response to any such danger.

The result of the above statements, I believe, is that the United States will continue the sale of defensive arms to Taiwan,[22] and also will strongly object to the use of force in the Taiwan area—essentially the same actions which could have been expected under the Mutual Defense Treaty.

Looking at United States-Taiwan relations as a whole, therefore, economic and cultural ties are not affected; our treaty relations remain unchanged except for the Mutual Defense Treaty; and the substantive security relations remain essentially the same. Some adjustments must be made in the manner in which we deal with Taiwan since there no longer are official relations. The United States has no embassy in Taipei, but instead operates through the American Institute on Taiwan; conversely, Taiwan is represented by the Coordinating Council for North American Affairs. These bodies are ostensibly private corporations. However, they are staffed by foreign service officers temporarily on leave, are funded by the respective governments, are entitled to certain privileges and immunities accorded foreign representatives and organs, and carry out an assortment of familiar "governmental" activities such as processing visas and taking depositions.[23]

C. The Status of Taiwan

After January 1, 1979 we know what the United States does *not* regard Taiwan to be: it is not the de jure government of the state of China. Much less clear, however, is the question of what the United States considers Taiwan to be.

The Taiwan Relations Act does not directly address this issue. The report of the Senate Committee on Foreign Relations states:

Considerable discussion has occured concerning the status of Taiwan under international law. The Committee concluded that it was unnecessary, in drafting this legislation, to address this issue since, for purposes of United States

22   On arms sales to Taiwan, see S. Rep. No. 7, 96th Cong., 1st Sess. 16-17 (1979).
23   Taiwan Relations Act §§ 6-13, 22 U.S.C. §§ 3305-3312 (Supp. III 1979).

domestic law, the Executive Branch can be empowered, statutorily, to treat Taiwan as if it were a state. This is, in fact, precisely what the bill does. . . .[24]

Thus, the United States has not explicitly explained the legal rationale for preserving treaties and maintaining commercial, cultural, and other relations with an unrecognized entity.

The successor government theory provides one possible rationale. That is, the United States has treaty and other relations with the state of China. Prior to January 1 that state was represented by the ROC government. After the switch of recognition the United States regards the PRC as the successor government to the ROC. As such, the PRC assumes the rights and obligations of its predecessor. This theory is well known. For example, in 1971 the PRC was recognized by the United Nations as the only legitimate representative of China, and succeeded to the seat belonging to that state.[25]

Some scholars argue that the successor government theory should be applied to the switch in recognition to the PRC.[26] But such an approach would produce some highly unsatisfactory results. First, the PRC would succeed to the Mutual Defense Treaty and other agreements with the United States. These treaties would remain in force only as long as the PRC agrees, in an implied manner, that they should continue to serve as the bases of American relations with the Chinese territory of Taiwan. This means that China could withdraw its implied agreement at any time and terminate American treaty relations with Taiwan. Second, the United States would be in the absurd situation of having a mutual defense treaty with the PRC for the purpose of defending Taiwan from being attacked by the PRC.

In addition, since the PRC would be the sole legitimate government of all of China including Taiwan, the United States could have no direct relations with the authorities on Taiwan without the PRC's

---

24   S. Rep. No. 7, 96th Cong., 1st Sess. 17 (1979).
25   26 U.N. GAOR, Supp. (Agenda Item 93), U.N. Doc. A/RES/2758 (1971), *reprinted in* Dep't St. Bull., vol. 65, no. 1690, p. 556 (Nov. 15, 1971). *See generally* Jerome Cohen & Hungdah Chiu, People's China and International Law 267-91 (1974).
26   *See, e.g.,* Jerome Cohen, *Normalizing Relations with the People's Republic of China,* A.B.A.J., vol. 64, no. 7, p. 940 (July 1978); *Legal Implications of Recognition of the People's Republic of China,* Am. Soc'y of Int'l L., Proceedings of the 72nd Annual Meeting 240 (1978).

consent, even if that consent is only implied. Taiwan would have no capacity to conduct foreign affairs unless the PRC consented.

A second possible description of the legal status of Taiwan after withdrawal of recognition is that it is a "de facto entity with international personality." That is, while no longer regarded by the United States as a de jure government or state, nevertheless Taiwan continues to control a population and territory and to carry out the usual functions of government. Section 4 of the *Restatement, Second, Foreign Relations Law of the United States* provides:

> Except as otherwise indicated, "state" as used in the Restatement of this Subject means an entity that has a defined territory and population under the control of a government and that engages in foreign relations.[27]

In other words, whether Taiwan is regarded as a "state" or juridical person in international law depends on whether it carries out the usual functions of a state, and not whether it is recognized de jure by other states.[28]

If Taiwan is a de facto entity with international personality, it may carry out the full range of foreign relations, including entering into international agreements and sending and receiving official missions.

The de facto entity concept is not a new idea. Prior to January 1, 1979, the United States dealt with the PRC on exactly such a basis. Although we did not extend de jure recognition to the PRC, official missions were exchanged, agreements were reached, American presidents visited the PRC, and a considerable amount of trade and travel was carried out between the two countries. No one seriously questioned the capacity of the PRC to engage in such relations.

I should note that this concept does not violate the principle of one-China. It addresses the present political realities without requiring or precluding eventual reunification or any other ultimate relationship between the PRC and Taiwan. Indeed, Vice-Premier Teng's

---

27   Similarly, article 1 of the Convention of Rights and Duties of States, 49 Stat. 3097, T.S. No. 881 (1933) says: "The state as a person of international law should possess the following qualifications: (a) a permanent population; (b) a defined territory; (c) government; and (d) capacity to enter into relations with other states."

28   It should be noted that approximately 20 states still recognize the ROC as the de jure government of the state of China.

indication that Taiwan may retain its own political and economic system as well as maintain separate armed forces acknowledges the same realities.[29]

The United States Position

The PRC obviously views the switch of recognition as a successor government situation. In its unilateral statement of December 15, 1978 the Chinese government said:

> As is known to all, the Government of the People's Republic of China is the sole legal government of China and Taiwan is part of China. . . . As for the way of bringing Taiwan back to the embrace of the motherland and reunifying the country, it is entirely China's internal affair.[30]

The United States has not taken a definitive stand on the status of Taiwan. In the Joint Communique of December 15, 1978, the United States "acknowledges the Chinese position that there is but one China and Taiwan is a part of China, [and] recognizes the People's Republic of China as the sole legal government of China. Within this context, the people of the United States will maintain cultural, commercial, and other unofficial relations with the people of Taiwan."[31]

One possible interpretation of these statements is that the PRC is the successor government to the ROC: The state of China includes Taiwan, and the PRC is the sole legal government of this state. Moreover, since the United States can deal with Taiwan only "within this context," the United States acknowledges the PRC's ultimate legal authority over Taiwan, including the right to approve future U.S.-Taiwan relations.

An alternative interpretation is that "acknowledgement" of the Chinese position is not tantamount to accepting it. Consequently, the United States still retains the options of regarding the status of

---

29 Senate Comm. on Foreign Relations, 96th Cong., 1st Sess., Sino-American Relations: A New Turn, 3-4 (Comm. Print 1979).
30 See appendix 6.
31 See appendix 4.

Taiwan as still "undetermined,"[32] dealing with it as a de facto entity with international personality, or at a later point explicitly accepting the PRC as the successor government to the ROC.

The word "acknowledge" presents a potentially serious linguistic discrepancy between the English and Chinese texts. The Shanghai Communique states: "The United States acknowledges that Chinese on both sides of the Strait agree that there is but one China and Taiwan is part of China. We do not challenge this position."[33] The Chinese text uses a correct equivalent, *jen-shih*, for "acknowledges." In the December 15 communique "acknowledges" is rendered in Chinese as *ch'eng-jen*, a term carrying a clear connotation of acceptance or agreement. Reading the Chinese texts of the two communiques together, the United States has increased the degree of its acquiescence in the Chinese position from *jen-shih* (acknowledges or takes note) to *ch'eng-jen*. Administration officials have stated that, in interpreting this phrase, the United States will adhere only to the English version.[34] Of course, China will adhere only to the Chinese version.

The United States may derive some short-term benefits from refusing to clarify its legal rationale for continued dealings with Taiwan. Explicitly calling Taiwan a de facto entity might annoy the PRC, while adopting the successor government theory would damage Taiwan. Nevertheless this policy of intentional ambiguity will be difficult to maintain for an indeterminate time.

Indeed, a great deal already has occurred which requires the United States to be increasingly specific about its view of the status of Taiwan. For example, Taiwan has deposited in American banks several billion dollars of its foreign exchange reserves. If the PRC were considered the successor government, it could assert that this money belongs to the "state of China" and should be handed over to

---

32   For a historical review and legal analysis of Taiwan's "undetermined" status, see *Normalization of Relations with the People's Republic of China: Practical Implications: Hearings Before the Subcomm. on Asian and Pacific Affairs of the House Comm. on International Relations*, 95th Cong., 1st Sess. 215, 219-24 (1977) (statement of Dr. Hungdah Chiu, Professor of Law, University of Maryland Law School).

33   See appendix 3.

34   S. Rep. No. 7, 96th Cong., 1st Sess. 9 (1979).

the proper representative of that state, the PRC. The transfer of this vast sum would undercut any policy of ensuring that the people of Taiwan "face a peaceful and prosperous future."[35]

The Taiwan Relations Act deals with this problem by providing in section 4(b)(3)(B) that the PRC does not succeed to the property of the ROC:

> [R]ecognition of the People's Republic of China shall not affect in any way the ownership of or other rights or interests in properties, tangible and intangible, and other things of value, owned or held on or prior to December 31, 1978, or thereafter acquired or earned by the governing authorities on Taiwan.[36]

A related problem which is not completely resolved concerns the ownership of the former ROC embassy at Twin Oaks and other diplomatic and consular properties. The Senate version of the Act excluded diplomatic real property from the application of the section quoted above, and hence would have supported the taking over of Twin Oaks by the PRC.[37] The Act, however, follows the House version, the legislative history of which indicates that this section applies to all property including diplomatic real property.[38]

The PRC considers obtaining the state of China's diplomatic property to be an important symbolic act. The Executive for political reasons may want to allow this property to pass to the PRC. Ultimately, the courts may have to decide whether the PRC is the successor government to the ROC, and, if so, whether section 4(b)(3)(B) should be narrowly construed so that it is consistent with international law rules regarding the rights of successor governments.[39]

The issue of whether the PRC is the successor government to the ROC will recur repeatedly in the future. For example, under what structure will athletes from the PRC and Taiwan participate in the Olympic Games? What are Taiwan's rights and obligations under

---

35 *United States Statement Accompanying the Joint Communique, December 15, 1978,* Dep't St. Bull., vol. 79, no. 2022, p. 26 (Jan. 1979); see appendix 5.
36 *See also* S. Rep. No. 7, 96th Cong., 1st Sess. 27 (1979).
37 *Id.*
38 H.R. Rep. No. 26, 96th Cong., 1st Sess. 10 (1979).
39 *See generally* Marjorie Whiteman, Digest of International Law, vol.2, pp. 904-15 (1963).

20

bilateral and multilateral international agreements on civil aviation? If the PRC objects, can American commercial, cultural, and educational bodies legally have direct dealings with the Taiwan government? Each such question will require a specific response from the United States, which in turn will set a pattern of precedents for future dealings.

My guess is that in the coming months and years the United States will increasingly assert, although with some reluctance, that Taiwan is a de facto entity with international personality. This formulation is awkward both semantically and substantively. But since both the PRC and Taiwan agree on the principle of one-China, it is hardly appropriate for the United States, as an outsider, to propose any other position. Having to operate within this principle, the United States must use the de facto entity concept if it is to maintain economic, cultural, and other ties with Taiwan into the indefinite future.

D. Relations with the PRC After Normalization

It should be emphasized that normalization is not the equivalent of friendship. Normalization merely removes the abnormal condition of non-recognition.

Clearly, there are a number of areas where the United States and China have parallel interests and therefore will cooperate with each other. Hopefully, these areas will grow in the future. In the past several years much stress has been placed on our parallel interests, in part by various administrations seeking support for their China policy. But we also must recognize that there will be times when our national interests differ. China's invasion of Vietnam in early 1979 is a dramatic case in point. Consequently, after normalization the United States will cooperate with China where we can, but we also must disagree where we should.

The Vietnam invasion also should remind us that while the Chinese leadership appears moderate on some matters, it is decidedly rigid in others. Moreover, given the history of wide political swings in China, we must at least consider the possibility that policies may change once again in the future. There must be at least a few people in China wondering about the appropriateness of disco dancing, Coca-Cola, and Pierre Cardin see-through blouses.

More seriously, we might ask whether the present modernization drive in China is going too far too fast. Is China able to absorb and utilize the considerable amount of new technology and equipment being introduced? We may be unable to answer these questions, but I believe that they are precisely the questions being asked inside China, and that these issues are partly responsible for the Spring 1979 slowdown in foreign trade, investment, and other dealings with the outside.

In addition, I do not think that the Cultural Revolution and other aspects of the radical left line in China were the personal handiwork of only Chairman Mao and a few top leaders. I think that their egalitarian, anti-elitist, romantic appeal struck a responsive chord in a number of people. It would not be overly surprising if at some point these people attempt to reassert the importance of Maoist ideological values, even at the price of slowing down modernization. They may not succeed. But we should not let our own preferences for modernization and pragmatism lead us to think that such preferences are "natural" and hence that all Chinese support these policies.

Lest I paint a too disturbing picture of radical change in the PRC, let me describe a second and more likely series of developments which argue for considerable stability in future United States-China relations.[40]

In 1970 the Chinese leadership made a broad reassessment of the international situation. The United States was withdrawing from Vietnam and, indeed, pulling back from all of Asia. The United States was rapidly declining as a serious immediate threat to China's international security. At the same time, the Soviet Union was becoming a substantial threat. The great increase in Soviet troops along the Chinese border, the border clashes of 1969, the dispatch of Soviet troops into Czechoslovakia, and the promulgation of the Brezhnev doctrine of limited sovereignty must have made the Chinese leadership very apprehensive about the Soviet Union.

A series of fundamental decisions was reached, all centered around national security concerns, that has shaped Chinese policies in this decade. I believe that these policies were supported by the

---

40   For a detailed discussion of this argument, see China's Quest for Independence: Policy Evolution in the 1970s (Thomas Fingar & Stanford Journal of International Studies eds., 1980), particularly the chapters by Fingar, Harding, Lewis, and Fenwick.

entire spectrum of political opinion, including the radical left. Even when the "gang of four" began to press its attacks in 1972-73 and 1975-76, its criticisms were directed more at how policies were being implemented than at the policies themselves.

One basic policy direction is that the Soviet Union has replaced the United States as the principal threat and enemy. One consequence of this policy has been that China played its "America card" in an effort to use the United States as a counterweight to Soviet power.

At the same time, China had to upgrade its military sector rapidly and substantially so that it could successfully defend against modern Soviet weapons. In order to do so, however, its entire scientific and technological infrastructure first had to be modernized. This effort has broad implications for Chinese society: A push for modernization might improve the population's standard of living as well as upgrade the military, but modernization also has side effects—increased dependence on foreign goods and technology, a growth of elitism, and a renewed stress on material incentives, among others—which might bend or stretch Maoist ideological values. Nevertheless, the needs of national security were considered so overriding that some of the social dangers of modernization had to be accepted. Additionally, it could not be known how long the "America card" would remain effective. Prudent leadership requires trying to modernize as quickly as possible, even at the risk of rushing forward pell-mell.

These basic considerations of the Sino-Soviet-United States triangle and of the need for rapid modernization remain essentially unchanged today, and they are likely to continue into the foreseeable future. Under this analysis, Chinese foreign policy also will remain essentially unchanged, regardless of which individual or group is in control.

II

The PRC and Reunification

Stephen: *The PRC policies of consulting the Taiwanese people and taking into consideration the present political and economic realities on Taiwan can be traced to Chou En-lai's discussions with the second and third Tiaoyutai delegations in 1972.* [1] *Last year, Vice-Premier Teng said to Senator Glenn that if Taiwan agrees to the principle of reunification, it could keep its army as well as its own political and economic system.* [2] *I think Teng's statement was a big step beyond what Chou En-lai prescribed.*

Thomas: The PRC position can be summarized in several main points. First and foremost, Taiwan Province is part of China, and therefore the Taiwan problem is an internal Chinese affair. In more recent statements, the PRC has declared that in the course of solving the Taiwan problem, it will consult the people on Taiwan and also will take into consideration the present political and economic realities. Toward these ends, the PRC will encourage postal communication, commercial relationships, and mutual visits by family members. Finally, the PRC has said that it will try to use peaceful means to solve the Taiwan problem, but at the same time will not relinquish its right to use other than peaceful means. Vice-Premier Teng recently

---

1   Joseph Lee, *Peking's View of Taiwan: An Interview with Chou En-lai,* in Taiwan's Future 65-70 (Yung-hwan Jo ed. 1974).
2   Senate Comm. on Foreign Relations, 96th Cong., 1st Sess., Sino-American Relations: A New Turn (Comm. Print 1979).

indicated two circumstances under which the non-peaceful measures might be used: If Taiwan tries to become an independent state, or if it tries to establish some kind of alliance with the Soviet Union.[3]

William: What does the phrase "take into consideration the present political and economic realities" mean? My difficulty is not with the idea itself, but rather with what it means in actual practice.

So far, there has been very little detailed explanation. For example, a stated policy is that the standard of living in Taiwan will not be lowered after reunification. How can this be achieved?

Charles: The PRC does face problems in trying to deal with the details of how to reunify China. One of the difficulties is that in the process of forming these policies, it has to consult the people on Taiwan. Consultation is just beginning, and so at this point we cannot expect much information about the details.

William: This explanation creates a chicken and egg problem. The PRC wants to consult the people on Taiwan before making these decisions, but consultations are not possible because contacts are highly limited at this point, and there will not be extensive contacts until after the people on Taiwan have committed themselves to reunification on Peking's terms. I can see someone in Taiwan saying that until he knows the precise terms of reunification, he cannot make any kind of commitment. How does one break this circle?

Robert: I share the view that the statements of the PRC are not specific enough. But, at the same time, I think the PRC also understands its dilemma. Right now it has only limited contact with native Taiwanese.

A. "... the PRC is trying to reach only the power-holders in the KMT, and not the Taiwanese people."

Frank: I am not convinced that the PRC actually intends to consult with the people on Taiwan. Although it repeatedly uses the phrase *tang-chia tso-chu* [to be the master of one's own fate] to describe its Taiwan policy, over the past decade there has been no evidence whatsoever that the PRC leadership has been trying to get the

---

3   *Peking Says Taiwan Can Keep Autonomy Under Unification,* New York Times, Jan. 10, 1979, at A8, col. 5.

opinions of the Taiwanese. The principal effort has been to contact the Nationalist leadership on Taiwan. Hence, the concept of consultation is not really convincing to the general public on Taiwan.

Stephen: As a number of Taiwanese have pointed out, PRC broadcasts to Taiwan and articles about Taiwan are the work of defected KMT officials appealing to their former colleagues and brethren. From the content of the broadcasts one can also see that the PRC is trying to reach only the power-holders in the KMT, and not the Taiwanese people.

The Taiwanese people are very disappointed that the Mainland authorities want to deal only with the KMT and are not concerned with the people. The PRC is not really trying to consult the people and does not care how the people really feel.

Henry: May I comment on that point? For the past six months I have been making trips around the country talking to Taiwanese. They tell me that they do not feel that they are being consulted or contacted by the PRC in any meaningful way.

I can give you an example. The Taiwanese Association of America [*Taiwan t'ung-hsiang-hui*] has a membership of approximately 100,000 in the United States—a very large organization. When Vice-Premier Teng was in Washington, D.C., on January 29, the Association wanted to meet with him and learn what the PRC sees for the future of Taiwan. A letter was written requesting a meeting. To our disappointment, about two weeks later, we received a response that he was too busy to meet with us. I can understand that, but I would have hoped that the request would be transferred to someone else. If the PRC is sincere about wanting to consult with the Taiwanese people, there are 100,000 in this Association who want to be consulted.

Moreover, there were reports around January 2 that Vice-Premier Teng sent congratulations to Chiang Ching-kuo for continuing to assert that Taiwan is part of China, thereby preventing Taiwan from becoming an independent state.[4] This action again pointed out to the Taiwanese people that the PRC authorities are only interested in government-to-government contact with the Taiwan authorities.

---

4   *Message to Taiwan Compatriots,* Beijing Review, no. 1, pp. 16-17 (Jan. 5, 1979), see appendix 11.

Robert: As far as I know, Vice-Premier Teng did meet with various groups of Taiwanese in Washington, Houston, and Atlanta. Why he selected one group rather than others I do not know.

Charles: From the Chinese point of view, the Taiwan problem is a domestic issue. It would have been undiplomatic for Teng to engage in domestic politicking while in the United States. He came to deal with U.S.-China relations.

Moreover, Ambassador Chai Zemin [PRC ambassador to Washington] has said that he would like to meet with Taiwanese people. Has this Association tried to meet with him? People who are really interested in talking with Chinese officials are able to do so.

James: When Ambassador Chai went to Boston, the Association asked to meet with him. He agreed to a meeting, but finally the appointment was cancelled by officials of the Association. I do not know why. In addition, contacts between lower-echelon officials and Taiwanese people have been going on for some time.

Henry: From what I know, Mr. Chai did not show up for the meeting, but instead a very low echelon representative came. He was not even considered official enough to be able to convey the results of conversations back to the PRC. That was why the meeting was called off.

James: I want to make some observations about why the PRC appeals to KMT officials all the time and does not pay sufficient attention to the Taiwanese people. From the PRC's point of view, the KMT does maintain effective control over Taiwan. The only people who can solve the Taiwan problem are those in power in Taiwan—the KMT.

The PRC always says that it deals with the KMT with the ultimate purpose of promoting the well-being of the Taiwanese. Of course, that could be just propaganda, but I believe that the present policy of the PRC reflects more the state of unreadiness on its part to solve the so-called Taiwan problem than its lack of concern for the Taiwanese people.

Its present concerns are to preserve the status quo as much as possible and to prevent the Nationalist government from going independent or establishing closer ties with the Soviet Union. Because of these concerns, it would be very difficult for the PRC to give a detailed program describing how the present political and economic systems will be affected once unification is achieved. It is not prepared to deal with the problem at this point.

I personally believe unification will come about under the following conditions. First, there must be military preparedness on the part of the PRC so that it has the capability to use force to take over Taiwan should that prove necessary. Force need not be used, but military readiness is an underlying precondition. Secondly, something must occur to compel the PRC to make up its mind to take action, either military or otherwise, to force the Taiwan authorities into submission or into negotiations. Third, there must not be a substantial risk of military confrontation with major powers as the PRC moves ahead on solving the Taiwan problem. Finally, the PRC will need strong support from the residents of Taiwan, at least in the form of public opinion. The PRC is not adequately prepared in this last regard—further evidence that it is not yet ready to solve the problem of Taiwan. From my point of view, only if these four conditions are met will the PRC take action on Taiwan.

Albert: I agree that the PRC is in no hurry. It feels that time is on its side. Of course, if some disruptive action were to occur, such as Taiwan declaring independence, that would change the whole ball game.

I think the Chinese leaders are playing a game with respect to the Taiwan issue. They are genuinely afraid that at some point the KMT will declare independence. Everybody knows that at this time the PRC cannot militarily invade Taiwan. An invasion would also disrupt political relations with the United States.

B. *". . . how is the PRC going to appeal to the Taiwanese people?"*

Philip: When I was in China, I raised the question of what is meant by taking into consideration the higher social and economic conditions. The Chinese officials responded, "Well, look at Shanghai. The bourgeoisie continue to preserve their way of life there. The standard of living is higher than in other parts of China. After reunification Taiwan will be given a period of time in which to adjust its socioeconomic conditions to those of China, although eventually it would become a part of the social and economic system of China."

Yet at this point I do not think that Peking can make a convincing argument to those living on Taiwan that they can accept some "Shanghai arrangement" during a transition period.

On the political side, how is the PRC going to appeal to the Taiwanese people? If unification with the PRC is to take place, many Taiwanese clearly would desire more political freedom than has been allowed by the KMT regime. But the political alternative that Peking offers is far from acceptable not only to the Taiwanese but also to the Chinese on the Mainland. What has happened to Tibet since the PRC's amalgamation is a warning signal to Taiwanese. The Tibetan people have not been consulted or been allowed to determine their own fate. The policy of *tang-chia tso-chu* strikes me as empty words.

I feel that if the PRC does not abandon it's stated principle of unification, it will have little choice but to resort to some kind of economic or military sanctions in order to subjugate Taiwan. I do not see the possibility of peaceful negotiations in the foreseeable future. The KMT will not be willing to negotiate its own surrender. I also do not see the majority of people in Taiwan rising up to assert a preference for Peking's rule.

So the question remains whether Peking values the principle of unification enough to pay a costly price to conquer Taiwan by force. Maybe one thing we concerned intellectuals can do is to induce the leaders in Peking to think about how much will unification contribute to the wealth, power, and prestige of China. Is the satisfying of an emotional desire for national unification worth such a great cost in human lives and material destruction?

Edward: There is another problem. Let us say that the PRC spells out in detail its policies toward Taiwan and gives guarantees to the Taiwanese people and to the KMT officials. Is this sufficient to reassure the people whose family and friends have been jailed and killed in China? How is it going to inspire confidence in the Taiwanese people, who have no sense of political identification with mainland China, that these promises will be kept? The Communists have made various guarantees in the past concerning land reform, step-by-step collectivization, and to the national bourgeoisie, and have broken them all. In view of its record on keeping promises, the PRC confronts a critical question of credibility.

Charles: After reunification the Taiwanese will not be dominated by mainland China, as Taiwan has been since the KMT took over in 1945. The Taiwanese themselves would be participants in the process of liberation. In this kind of relationship, do not underestimate the political awareness of the Taiwanese people. If Taiwanese are mistreated after reunification, they will still be able to protest, just like what occurred in Tienanmen Square.

No one can guarantee your freedom. The real guarantee is the political awareness of the Taiwanese people. I do not see the possibility under the KMT regime for political education and the raising of political awareness; I do see that possibility under a Communist or socialist regime.

C. *". . . the PRC is still learning about the situation in Taiwan."*

Frank: What is the PRC's perception of the current situation in Taiwan? What does it understand about Taiwan in terms of political orientation, economic system, or class structure?

James: Personally, I think the PRC is still learning about the situation in Taiwan. I do not think that at this point the Chinese leaders have a very clear understanding of the aspirations of the local people on Taiwan. It is precisely this lack of understanding that has led the PRC to take a very low-keyed position on the details of unification. Given time, it will learn more about Taiwan.

Robert: One recent example of the PRC's view of the situation in Taiwan is the statement issued last month concerning the opposition politicians in Taiwan, particularly the Yu Teng-fa case.[5] The PRC said that the Nationalist authorities' suppression of Yu and other opposition people is not justified, and that Yu's view on reunification should be respected. In general, the PRC urges the people on Taiwan to express their views, and asserts that actions of people like Yu indicate the people's dissatisfaction with the KMT.

William: Is the PRC's perception of the views of Yu and other opposition politicians on reunification correct?

Robert: Yu stated quite clearly in an interview in a book published in the United States, *Tang-wai ti sheng-yin*, [Non-Party Voices], that he strongly advocates the unification of China. I think it was because of this that he was imprisoned. He also made some comments about the Taiwan independence movement, saying that independence is not possible and is not in line with the traditional view of people in Taiwan.

---

5   *Taiwan Authorities Must Stop Persecuting the People on Taiwan*, Chung-kuo hsin-wen-she [China News Service], May 7, 1979 (in Chinese).

There were many interviews with people in that book. The interviewer was Wang To, a writer who was a candidate for office during the last election.

Henry: I would like to make some comments about the Yu case. All of us understand the situation in Taiwan. People can talk about reunification, since that is one of the approved national policies. But to speak of independence is tantamount to committing a crime.

In order to avoid trouble, the opposition politicians prefer to talk about reunification instead of independence. The rationale is that reunification can be understood as reunifying with mainland China under the system of democracy rather than Communism. We have to be very careful in interpreting these words.

Question: How do you respond to Yu's specific statement that he is against independence?

Henry: You have to understand Wang To's background. I think it is quite easy for the interviewer to inject his own opinion in the course of interviewing someone else. What Mr. Yu said could somehow have been manipulated.

Question: Are you saying that Yu's statement that he is against independence should be attributed to Wang To?

Henry: That is a possibility. I may have overstated my point, which is that if a person in Taiwan had something in mind about independence, he would cover it up and phrase it in terms of reunification.

That is why I emphasize that the future of Taiwan should be decided by a national plebiscite. It should not depend on political views of individuals such as Mr. Yu.

Matthew: The PRC and the ROC agree on one point: they both want unification. Consequently, the statement that Yu was arrested because he favored unification is clearly a distortion. The PRC tried to make it seem as if he endorsed the PRC's position, whereas his statement really did not conflict with the ROC's position either. The PRC made this distortion in an effort to sow confusion.

Stephen: I think it is a mistake for the PRC to try to make a case out of the fact that Yu is in favor of reunification. The real reasons for his arrest are that he is a symbol of political opposition to KMT rule, and he was going to organize an opposition party.

D. *". . . there was no question in anybody's mind that Taiwan
. . . should automatically go back to China."*

Charles: The relationship between Taiwan and China is historical,
cultural, and racial. It is different from Taiwan's relations with
Japan or the United States. Some people in Taiwan do believe they
are a part of China. They want to reunify with China—I said reunify
rather than unify—not because China is more powerful or better off
economically or politically. Even if China were having problems,
some people would still feel that they are part of China.

Robert: I have very vivid memories from my childhood on Taiwan
when my parents and grandparents thought of themselves as
Chinese, socially, politically, and culturally.

When Taiwan was recovered from the Japanese, the people on
Taiwan wholeheartedly welcomed the people from the Mainland. This
is fully documented. The anti-KMT sentiment is something more
recent. The term "Taiwan independence movement" did not come
into use until after the February 28, 1947 massacre by the KMT.

Stephen: There is no question that in 1945 people were exuberant
over liberation from Japanese rule, and enthusiastically welcomed
the return of Taiwan to China.

But I think the real question is this: Do the Taiwanese people not
have the right to become politically independent at some later date
just because the Taiwanese people are ethnically and culturally
Chinese and because Taiwan was returned to China in 1945? The PRC
emphasizes that because Taiwan historically belongs to China and
because the people there are ethnically Chinese, Taiwan must remain
within the Chinese political entity. Is this argument convincing?
Austria and Germany, as well as the United States and England,
come from the same origins, but all are separate countries. The
question of whether or not there is a right for one part of a country to
break off and form a separate state is really a function of political
power and is not dependent on abstract theory.

Vincent: The "greater China syndrome" has long been an important
part of Chinese life. I remember during the war with Japan and in the
years immediately after victory there was no question in anybody's
mind that areas such as Taiwan, the Pescadores, and Shantung
province should automatically go back to China. We had always been
taught to believe that these territories were taken away illegally, and
that they should be returned to China.

I suspect that most of the Chinese leaders, as well as most of the people on the Mainland, still feel the same way. The completion of the process has only been postponed 30 years because of Chiang Kai-shek's actions and American intervention. The Taiwan problem is a very emotional issue.

Matthew: This obsession with unification is a very peculiar Chinese tradition. The Chinese love to say that state, government, and civilization are all one. But we know things can be different. We can have people of different languages governed by the same government, the same nation divided into two states, and several nations sharing one civilization. This is a uniquely Chinese problem, because the Chinese see the three concepts as indivisible.

David: Twins can be happy without living together. If living together means that they can help each other, that is a good reason for staying together. But if living together means being unhappy and fighting all the time, then they should live apart. Even husbands and wives who do not get along together should live apart.

Robert: I have all along wanted to see a united China. From a personal point of view, I have always had strong feelings about China and wanted to go back for a visit.

I know other people with similar feelings. There is a person whose family has been in Taiwan for over 300 years, yet he wanted to go visit his "native village" in China. After arriving in Canton, he asked to visit the place he knew only from his family geneological book. He did find that town from 300 years ago, and also learned that the whole village has the same surname as his own. There are people like that in Taiwan. I was brought up the same way.

Henry: There are so many different opinions and reactions. I also have a story to tell about a Taiwanese friend. While in Taiwan he was politically quite active, supporting the KMT. But, he soon changed his mind after going to study in Osaka. He then traveled to Peking for a short visit, and wrote me a letter saying that he hoped we could meet in Peking next year. This occurred about five years ago. When I received that letter I was quite surprised, because he had changed so quickly from supporting the KMT to promoting reunification on PRC terms.

Three years ago I received a letter from his wife in Osaka saying that he was having immigration problems in Japan and asking for help to bring the whole family to the United States. I could not do much for him since we were not relatives. The last thing I heard was that he was in jail in Japan for having overstayed his visa.

My point is that he was so enthusiastic about promoting reunification, but when he had to choose between going to jail or going to live in China, he chose jail. Yet he is the one who tried to convince me about reunification. If he does not have the guts to go settle in China himself, how can he convince the average person in Taiwan that it is better to spend his life under the Communist government?

E. ". . . *the people on Taiwan will have a better future as part of a united China.*"

Robert: I am greatly concerned about the welfare of the people on Taiwan. My family is still there, over a thousand people. I think that a unified China is in the interests of the people of Taiwan. The question is how to preserve the living standard of the people on Taiwan as unification moves forward. It is no secret that Taiwan's living standard is better than that of mainland China.

I genuinely believe that in the long run, the people of Taiwan will have a better future living as a part of a united China. You can make a analogy to the American Civil War. In the long run, the American people benefitted by remaining united.

We all know that the people on Taiwan are fearful about Communism. This is a result of 30 years of separation and the propaganda put out by the KMT. If you ask the people on Taiwan, "Do you like the PRC?" they are not able to answer; they know nothing about the PRC's policies and achievements.

I think the PRC's policy is now more realistic and practical than the policy of six or seven years ago. It is trying to alleviate the fears of the KMT. Of course, the KMT will say that guarantees by the Communists are not to be believed. In addition, the PRC also has to alleviate the concern of the Taiwanese that they are not adequately consulted and do not participate in the process of deciding Taiwan's future.

All along I have said that PRC policies toward Taiwan have not been specific enough, but they are getting more specific now and will become even more so in the future. I think that current policies encouraging personal and commercial contacts will increase understanding between these two groups. We will see a gradual process of people visiting back and forth and other forms of communication.

Vincent: I also feel that the present Peking policy toward Taiwan is pragmatic and realistic. Most of the Chinese leaders are not willing or able to say that they can live indefinitely with Taiwan as a separate entity. Taiwan is a constant reminder to the mainland Chinese that there is another way for the Chinese people.

But I also have to say that I think the PRC leaders are out of touch with the Taiwan situation. For 30 years they have listened to their own propaganda. They seem to think that the KMT rules over an unwilling and sullen Taiwanese people, and that the Taiwan economy is manipulated by the United States.

Now I realize that some people on the Mainland know better; I assume that they have up-to-date information about Taiwan. But I am worried that they interpret these facts to serve their own needs and in accordance with their own emotional blindness. I have a feeling that the leadership in Peking is not as much in touch with the Taiwan situation as we may give them credit for being.

III

The ROC and Reunification

Henry: *For the past 30 years the KMT regime has said that it would bring us back to mainland China. Can you tell me when this is going to happen? We have been waiting for 30 years. When will the ROC bring us back to mainland China?*

George: The ROC position is as follows: First, there is only one China. Second, there is only one legitimate government of China, the ROC. Third, the KMT is dead against the Taiwan independence movement, which is destructive and detrimental to the very survival of the ROC. Fourth, there will be no bilateral talks with the PRC, open or secret. Fifth, there will also be no communication with Peking and no commercial or cultural exchanges.

In addition, the Nationalists demand that China must be reunified, but under the condition that Marxism must go. Private ownership also must return, individual liberty and freedom must be guaranteed, and there must be no class struggle. These positions were made very clear by Premier Y.S. Sun.

With regard to the future political structure of Taiwan, prior to derecognition there was a commitment to holding elections for the Legislature and the National Assembly, and also to enlarging the number of seats up for election. But, of course, the situation changed with derecognition, and the elections have been suspended. I know the KMT must resume the elections, but when and under what terms is still subject to discussion. The party has set up a task force to consider this question.

With respect to the opposition, I think the Nationalists hold a deep apprehension about the motivation of these people who want to set up an opposition party. While such a step can serve some opposition purposes, it also can be exploited by Peking. Peking will try to do everything possible to subvert the present government, including manipulating an opposition party.

What is going to happen now that derecognition has occurred? The Nationalists have several objectives: to defend the security of Taiwan, to perfect Taiwan as a model for the future, and to regain the Mainland. They will accomplish these goals using a Chinese model following the Three-People's-Principles [*San-min chu-i*].[1] They see Peking as following an opposite path by basing itself on Western Marxism.

We should not underestimate the importance of the issue of models or cultural alternatives. Since the T'ung-chih restoration of 1860, there has been a 120-year effort to find the proper means for modernizing China. In the past 30 years we have seen two models operating under conditions of relative peace. For the first time, China has a chance to compare the Communist model used on the Mainland and the Three-People's-Principles model used on Taiwan.

Let me offer my personal views. In Chinese history there have been periods of unification and division. We are now in a transitional period. This is part of China's growing pains as it becomes modernized. China eventually will be unified. There is no Taiwan question; this is really a China question, a question about the modernization of China.

How long can the Nationalists go on like this? As I understand it, they are not going to give up without a last-ditch fight. I was present on one occasion when a top leader was asked, "In case there is an invasion, will you pack and go?" His answer was a flat "No." He would not leave Taiwan under any circumstances.

Edward: You say that the ROC is the only legitimate government of China. Presumably the basis of that legitimacy is the Constitution of 1947.[2] Yet the fact is that most of the provisions of the Constitution have been suspended by martial law, which has been in effect for over 30 years.[3] How can the KMT continue to base its legitimacy on a

---

1   *See* Sun Yat-sen, *San-min chu-i* (Frank Price trans., Shanghai 1927).
2   A Compilation of the Laws of the ROC, vol. 1, pp. 3-41 (Taipei 1967).
3   *Temporary Provisions Effective during the Period of Communist Rebellion, id.* at 43-44.

document that has been essentially suspended? The KMT says that it wants to bring that Constitution back to China to benefit the people of China, but it has never been practiced even on Taiwan.

I also want to ask you about the KMT's suspicion about efforts to organize an opposition party. We know that power tends to corrupt and absolute power tends to corrupt absolutely. Given a situation where the party in power prevents the formation of an opposition party that can articulate alternative views and serve as a watchdog, how do you prevent the party in power from being isolated from the people? How do you prevent corruption and greed?

As for the important KMT goal of recovering the Mainland, I can see that given the situation in which the KMT finds itself, this principle is an excellent self-serving justification for preserving minority rule. The KMT cannot even defend the off-shore islands in case of another crisis, much less try to retake the Mainland. In case of war, the KMT can count on the Taiwan conscripts to defend the Taiwan homeland, but I am not sure they will join the KMT officer corps to go to mainland China. George, you have talked to high-ranking officers in the Taiwan military; they must know the situation. Why do they keep saying they will recover the Mainland?

I know how they will answer you. They will reiterate what they have been saying for three decades—that recovery of mainland China from the Communists is a "sacred calling" of the KMT which is "the sole legitimate government of China," and that this calling must be carried out regardless of the cost or how long it will take. Of course they know better than that. They know that these policies are superb political rationales for justifying their rule and denying demands for change in the political status quo.

That much is clear to me. What puzzles me is the KMT's assessment of the cost of continued adherence to that political myth relative to the cost of abandoning it. In the wake of Nixon's visit to the PRC in 1972, continued adherence to that myth means foregoing some realistic and viable options which may enhance the prospect of the survival of a non-Communist Taiwan. Then why does the KMT continue to follow Chiang Kai-shek's dictum "to remain changeless in the face of changes and surprises?" I do not have an answer to this question. George, I am interested in listening to what you have to say.

George: I have no answers for some of these questions. Let me just speak here as an individual.

The Nationalists have been in power for a long time. The question now is how to share the power, and to do so in a way as to ensure that what they started will not become distorted. The Nationalists think that a China based on Sun Yat-sen's principles, imperfect though these may be, should have a chance to succeed. They want an opportunity to carry out that model. For the first time in Chinese history, Taiwan has become one of the centers for Chinese human resources. If Taiwan were a police state or a dictatorship, I do not think that it would dare to train so many highly educated scholars. We can compare what happened on the Mainland during the same period. There was a total attack on Chinese culture. It is not because they are not as smart as we are, but rather that the Chinese Communist regime did not give its potential scholars a chance. The so-called Great Cultural Revolution turned out to be the Catastrophic Cultural Revocation, a fact now officially admitted by the Communist regime itself.

A. *"Taiwan is not just a piece of real estate; there are 17 million people living there."*

Matthew: I want to point out that the PRC and ROC positions we have been discussing are the positions of the governments. The people have not yet been asked whether they want to have unification, or on what terms.

Lawrence: Who is it that desires unification? The KMT? China? Or the Taiwanese people? Taiwan is not just a piece of real estate; there are 17 million people living there. When you talk about unification, don't you think that it is morally necessary to get the consent of these people?

On what moral ground can China advocate unification? Taiwan has been separate from China for 80 years, except from 1945 to 1949. And during this four-year period Taiwan had a very bad experience with China, including the February 28 massacre.

There should be a plebiscite to let the people of Taiwan decide whether they want unification or not. Three alternatives should be presented. First, do you want the PRC to liberate Taiwan? Second, do you want the KMT to continue to rule Taiwan? Third, do you want the people on Taiwan to establish a government of their own in place of the KMT regime? As everybody knows, more than 90 percent of the people in Taiwan would choose the third alternative. I think that some of the Taiwanese here who favor unification know that. You are in touch with the sentiment of the Taiwanese.

Charles: I doubt very much indeed that 90 percent of the people in Taiwan favor independence. If you took a poll of Taiwanese capitalists, you may be right, but if you ask the peasants, I think you will reach a much different result.

William: I do not doubt that a very large percentage would choose Lawrence's third alternative if the questions were framed the way he suggests. But if they were broadened, first by adding that independence will almost surely trigger some drastic action by the PRC, possibly even war, and second, by posing the possibility of substantial reform by the KMT, then how would the people choose? If the choices were phrased in this way, I am not sure the majority would pick independence. From my contact with Taiwan, it seems to me that most people regard the preservation of economic prosperity and political stability as the key considerations.

   B. *"The Nationalist insistence upon the abandonment of Marxism may perform an important historical mission and a real service for China."*

Charles: George said that from the KMT point of view, this is not the time to talk about reunification with the PRC or to begin negotiations. I would just like to know: When is the right time to begin negotiations?

George: Premier Sun made very clear the conditions under which unification would be acceptable to Taiwan. The PRC should abandon Marxism and Maoism and restore private ownership and individual freedom to the people.

   I think such issues should be the preliminary grounds for discussion. I do not think the Nationalists can accept any proposal in which Marxism takes command. This would only mean surrender. We should not treat these conditions for negotiation as a farce or a joke. Many people's lives will be at stake. A lot of people believe these ideas, not just the Nationalists. There are a lot of Chinese around the world who agree with this position.

   If Peking insists on doing away with the flag, the anthem, and the title, there will be still more demands to come. I learned this as a student. What the Communists really are talking about is surrender. Each generation has to be newly reeducated about it.

Let me make an analogy. The Communists say that during World War II they did the fighting with Japan while the Nationalists paid attention only to fighting with the Communists. They forget what is an important Nationalist contribution to the war: The Nationalists did not surrender. They turned down a German proposal to surrender. But suppose they had surrendered? The eventual result of World War II would be anybody's guess.

The same thing is happening today. The Nationalists' insistence upon the abandonment of Marxism may perform a historical mission and a real service for China. This demand may not be very relevant to some people in this generation, but it may be an important contribution in an historical sense.

William: You have explained to us the formal rhetorical position of the ROC government, and I must say that I feel greatly dismayed. The ROC sets conditions for the beginning of negotiations that are just not going to be met. The people in the Taiwan government making these policies seem to think they are dealing from a position of strength. The truth is that Taiwan is in a lot of trouble. To set impossible threshold conditions for discussion with the PRC is not going to get Taiwan out of trouble.

Stephen: The ROC continues to claim to be the national government and says it wants to unify China. How can the ROC do it? People have talked about the possibility of a Sino-Soviet conflict in which China is defeated, and the ROC comes to help its Mainland compatriots resist the Russians. Another scenario entertained by many people in the ROC is that there will be warring factions within China, some of which may ally with Taiwan. Both seem rather remote possibilities.

I'd like to ask if these two scenarios sum up the ROC's thinking on how it might recover the Mainland. Do they imply that the ROC will be unable to recover the Mainland by its own efforts alone?

George: President Chiang Ching-kuo has said that at the present time there will be no development of nuclear weapons, but I personally would question that.

Lawrence: Let me just interject. The one thing I hate about the KMT regime is its lack of credibility. It says one thing but does another. People are urged to speak out because it is an open society, but when people speak out they are arrested. And now the same thing is happening with regard to nuclear weapons. Chiang Ching-kuo says he is not going to produce these weapons, but you seem to question that.

George: This is not hypocrisy. The public policy is not to develop nuclear weapons, but clearly there are people who think the weapons should be developed. What I doubt is whether the policy of no development of nuclear weapons can go on forever. At this time I do not think any one of us really knows what is going on in this area.

C. ". . . *while the KMT itself has a single position, not everyone in the party may feel the same way."*

Matthew: We should distinguish between the ROC's rhetorical position and what it will do in practice. The same distinction can be applied to the PRC. I think it knows that except in case of internal disturbance on Taiwan the PRC cannot take Taiwan without the loss of a few million lives. The PRC must also know that the issue of unification is heavily symbolic. There has to be some kind of pragmatism in the PRC as well. Unfortunately, visitors to the PRC, unlike visitors to Taiwan, cannot ask the kind of question that can find the pragmatic position behind the formal rhetoric.

We also should note that while the KMT itself has a single position, not everyone in the party may feel the same way. For example, while the ROC continues to refuse to talk to the PRC, there have been elements within the moderate wing of the KMT who did try to talk, using the Olympics issue as a vehicle. Some of these people felt that reaching a solution to the question of representation at the Olympics would be the beginning of the effort to face the reality of two regimes existing under the common name of China.

Let me try to describe the various groups within and outside the KMT more fully. In the past seven years, the question of the KMT's legitimacy has grown increasingly critical. After the events of last December, anybody who pays any attention to these matters knows that the KMT leaders realize they can no longer get away with merely trying to preserve the status quo. The question for the KMT regime is how to reform while preserving some continuity.

There are two schools of thought within the KMT on how to do this. One might be called the ultraconservative wing—of course these kinds of labels do not mean very much. Members of this school advocate Chinese cultural superiority; some are anti-Western, anti-democracy, and anti-modernization. This group is especially strong in the government, the security and military apparatus, the educational sector, and the media. Increasingly, it has been making an appeal to the younger generation. Many younger people are unhappy about the overemphasis on material things exhibited by some businessmen. This group wants change, but in its own particular way. For example, no constitutional changes will be made concerning the Legislature. But as members elected on the Mainland in 1947 die off, the vacancies will not be refilled. Consequently, over a period of time the Legislature will consist only of those elected on Taiwan. This group also wants reforms in the areas of social service and welfare. No legitimacy of any kind will be given the so-called opposition. The conservatives regard the opposition as traitors, and in fact publicly call its members traitors. The opposition, the Taiwan independence movement, and Communist agents are seen as three-in-one.

Another group of persons whom I would call the more genuine reformists compose the so-called liberal or moderate wing of the KMT. Its members are the businessmen, bankers, the managerial class, and persons who run state enterprises. Many of them have been educated in the Western tradition, if not necessarily in the West. By the nature of their functions, these technocrats must work with Taiwanese; in the course of doing so they have come to appreciate some of the patterns of the Taiwanese. This group wants some kind of reform within the KMT structure, but these reforms have to meet two conditions. First, any change has to assure the safety and psychological security of those already in power. The specific officeholders might change, but there also must be some kind of continuity. In addition, new positions have to be created to accomodate the new aspirations developing among people in Taiwan. The overall effect is that changes will occur, but in a manner preserving the continued dominance of politics by the KMT.

It is within this context that we should look at changes being introduced by the KMT. The working groups of the party central committee that were formed after the December 15 announcement are likely to propose programs of gradual change. In addition, there have been efforts to strengthen judicial independence. There also have been discussions about a new election law and even new elections. A proposal to abolish martial law was made, but was rejected. These kinds of schemes are basically KMT oriented and initiated, and are designed to continue KMT domination.

D. *". . . we must bear these new forces in mind."*

Philip: The opposition people are asking for much more fundamental change. They see the challenge to the KMT's legitimacy as real, profound, and already taking place. They argue that the situation will only get worse if the KMT does not make substantial changes.

In the past three or four years there has been a growing polarization in Taiwan politics. An example of the polarization is the Chungli incident of 1977, which was a mass protest against unfair KMT electoral practices. This incident indicates that new political forces have emerged, mainly from the generation that is in its thirties and forties. These people have widespread grassroots contacts and are different from the older type of opposition politicians such as Kao Yu-shu and Kuo Yu-hsin. The new group is as well-educated, but is more modern and more internationally oriented. Many of them are economically independent, if not wealthy, and do not have to depend on the government for their survival.

The mainstream of the opposition movement in Taiwan centers around Hsu Hsin-liang, Yao Chia-wen, Huang Hsin-chieh, and Lin I-hsiung. Wang To is to their left and Chang Chun-hung and Kang Ning-hsiang are to their right. I would not consider the mayor of Tainan, Su Nan-cheng, to be a member of the opposition. In effect, the opposition is a political coalition of various opponents of the KMT.[4]

Within the mainstream, Hsu represents those people who are concerned with social and economic reform for the lower income group. He studied in England, where he was influenced by the thinking of the Fabian Socialists and the British Laborites. There had been rumors that Hsu was politically leaning toward the left. In a recent newspaper interview, Hsu categorically rejected the idea

---

4   For details on the political views of these persons, see Hsu Hsin-liang, *Feng-yu chih sheng* [The Sounds of Wind and Rain] (Taipei 1978); Yao Chia-wen, *Hu-fa yu pien-fa* [Defending the Law and Changing the Law] (Taipei 1978); Lin I-hsiung, *Ts'ung Lan-yang tao Wu-feng* [From Lan-yang to Wu-feng] (Taipei 1978); Wang To, *Min-chung ti yen-ching* [The Eyes of the People] (Taipei 1978); Chang Chun-hung, *Wo-ti ch'eng-shih yu fen-tou* [My Methods and Struggles] (Taipei 1977); Kang Ning-hsiang, *Wen-cheng liu nien* [Six Years of Political Inquiry] (Taipei 1978); Su Nan-cheng, *Li-hsing ti hu-huan* [The Call of Reason] (Tainan 1977). Huang Hsin-chieh is the publisher of the journal *Mei-li-tao* [Beautiful Island].

of unification on anything like PRC terms.[5] He had established a
liaison between the mainstream of the opposition movement and
Chen Ku-ying and Wang To. In fact, Hsu's brother served as
campaign manager for Chen in the December, 1978 elections. In
order to counter these rumors, Hsu made a number of public
statements to clarify his position. Evidently, he remains highly
skeptical about the intentions of the PRC toward Taiwan, and also
appears to oppose the one-party dictatorship in PRC politics.

There are many thousands of persons in the opposition. It has 30
to 40 leading activists, each of whom has grassroots support and a
personal constituency among high school graduates, small businessmen, the new middle class, and so forth. These people are generating
a rising tide of political activity, and are using the issue of legitimacy
to assault the KMT.

What this means is that any discussion about reformist activities
on Taiwan must take into account the growing political polarization
between the KMT and the newly emerging opposition forces. We
cannot ignore this latter group of people. It also would solve no
problem to arrest all the opposition overnight. After all, there are
thousands of them. Refusal by the KMT to make any major concessions to them will lead to further political polarization, which may
in time lead to confrontation.

Many of the opposition activists have publicly stated that they
are ready to go to jail or even to die for their cause. They speak much
more daringly than many of us are talking here. Their campaign
speeches were unbelievably provocative.[6]

We must look at the future of Taiwan in a realistic manner. The
fact that the KMT remains a dominant political force cannot be
ignored. Any plan for political change would have to accommodate
the objectives of both the KMT leaders and the Taiwanese who have
joined their ranks and who will have much to lose if change is too
drastic. At the same time, we also recognize the existence of an

5   The interview appears in *Taiwan min-chu yun-tung hai-wai t'ung-men
     k'uai-hsin* [Bulletin of the Overseas Alliance for Democratic Rule in
     Taiwan], no. 14 (May 1979).
6   *See generally 1978 Taiwan tang-wai ching-hsuan ch'uan-tan chi* [Col-
     lection of 1978 Elections Materials of the Non-party Candidates in
     Taiwan] (published by Taiwan shu-wu, address unknown 1978).

emerging political opposition. If opposition demands are not given legitimate attention, political cleavage may intensify in the years ahead.

Frank: I don't know how many of you are aware of the incident involving the celebration of Hsu Hsin-liang's birthday, in which 30,000 people participated.[7] I was also surprised to see a declaration drafted by the Taiwan Human Rights Committee,[8] a group organized by Kang Ning-hsiang, who is considered a moderate compared to Hsu and others. Yet this organization issued a really strong statement saying that its members are willing to go to jail for their political beliefs.

The grassroots demand for greater political participation is not really an effort to boot out the KMT or remove the Mainlanders. It is a demand for equal participation. This kind of thing should be taken seriously.

George: I think that we have two separate issues here, a local one and a national one. The former involves questions such as whether the governor of Taiwan should be popularly elected. I personally see very little justification for why he is not.

The national issue is reunification with the Mainland. The KMT has never varied from the principle of reunification, but the question has always been reunification on what basis? Peking says reunification should be on the basis of upholding Marxism-Maoism and getting rid of the ROC. The ROC says no.

Vincent: But that is a negative statement of what Taiwan does not want. What does it want in a positive sense?

George: I earlier stated Premier Sun's conditions. I also want to stress that Taiwan should make itself into a model of development. It should gain a lot of time and also win the complete confidence of the people. Some people here tend to berate and condemn Chiang Ching-kuo. I can challenge every one of them. Even if there is an

---

7   *Over 30,000 People Participate in Chungli Political Gathering*, Hua-
     ch'iao jih-pao [Overseas Chinese Daily], Jun. 6, 1979 (in Chinese). Hsu
     Hsin-liang was magistrate of Tao-yuan county, and a leading opposition
     figure.

8   *We Are Willing to Go to Prison for Democracy in Taiwan*, id.

election, you cannot defeat him. Of course there are shortcomings on Taiwan. As an individual, I am going to address myself to them when I go there. I will press the issue. Taiwan should not remain in isolation, nor just say no to discussions and merely reject everything. It should make more aggressive demands and try hard to reach the majority of the people on the Mainland.

IV

The Taiwan Independence Movement

Lawrence: *Is the claim that people on Taiwan favor unification propaganda or reality? If it is reality, why does not China initiate a resolution in the United Nations calling for a plebiscite in Taiwan?*

Lawrence: I was born in Taiwan. I consider myself Taiwanese, not Chinese. I have never been in China, and my father and grandfather have never been in China. I think that Taiwan belongs to the Taiwanese. The United States, the PRC, and the ROC cannot determine the future of Taiwan. Only the Taiwanese can determine their own future.

The Chiang Ching-kuo regime represents nobody except themselves. They do not represent the Chinese people; they were kicked out by the Chinese people 30 years ago. They also do not represent the Taiwanese, because there has been no general nationwide election in Taiwan.

Let me turn to the current political situation in Taiwan. The basic policy of the government in Taiwan is the recovery of the Mainland. The KMT made this policy by itself; the Taiwanese have never participated in the decision.

When you ask the KMT, "Why do you want to recover the Mainland?", it answers that it wants to implement the Three-People's-Principles on the Mainland. But to what extent have these principles been implemented in Taiwan in the past 30 years?

The first is the principle of People's Democracy.[1] According to Sun Yat-sen, the purpose of this principle is to protect minority peoples. If that is the case, the KMT should cut its diplomatic relations with South Africa, the most oppressive government in the world. South Africa was expelled from the United Nations because of its racial policies, but the KMT maintains very, very good relations with that country. This is evidence that the KMT has betrayed the principle of People's Democracy.

The second principle is People's Livelihood. Sun Yat-sen said that the purpose of this principle is to promote the livelihood of all the people. Let us see if the KMT actually does this. Everybody knows that the richest person in Taiwan is Wang Yung-Ching. He is a billionaire, although 20 years ago he was extremely poor. The KMT system works against the principle of People's Livelihood by allowing the concentration of great wealth and by not supporting the well-being of the ordinary people. Strikes in Taiwan are outlawed, so a worker is paid only what the management wants to give him. Wages and working conditions for workers on Taiwan are extremely poor. I do not have to waste my time explaining this; it is well known.

The third principle is People's Power. Let us talk about the right to participate in the governmental process. In the national legislature, the people on Taiwan have only 5-10 percent of the representation. In the cabinet only four out of about 20 persons are Taiwanese, while the others are Chinese. As you know, Taiwanese constitute 85 percent of the population on Taiwan. Moreover, all first deputy ministers are Chinese. All the high civil service officials, military commanders, district military commanders, and police chiefs are Chinese. At the provincial level, the governor is appointed by the central authorities, as are the mayors of Taipei and Kaohsiung. So we cannot elect officials at the provincial or the national level.

You can see that we are ruled by a very small minority of Chinese people who occupy all of the key positions in the society and in the government.

---

1   The Three-People's-Principles are usually rendered as the principles of nationalism (*min-chu*), democracy (*min-ch'uan*), and livelihood (*min-sheng*).

What about freedom of speech and freedom of association? As you know, many books cannot be published or distributed on Taiwan. If you have read *Taiwan cheng-lun* [Taiwan Political Review, a journal banned in 1975] or *Hsuan-chu wan-sui* [Long Live Elections] you know that there is nothing wrong with them; nevertheless the government cannot tolerate freedom of speech even to this extent.

I read the newspapers in Taiwan very carefully, and I am bothered by what I see. Chiang Ching-kuo often says that this is an open society that encourages criticism. Yet when some people really try to criticize the government, they end up in jail. In China, at least they openly say that they are going to exercise proletarian dictatorship and will restrict the freedom of speech. But Taiwan does the same thing while claiming to be an open and democratic society. This is extremely immoral.

If the KMT is really committed to democracy, the people should have the rights to organize and to assemble, including forming political parties. Why cannot the people in Taiwan organize political parties?

Let us talk about human rights in Taiwan. I am convinced that many people have been arrested and tortured very badly by the KMT. One example is Hsieh Ts'ung-min. He was arrested on February 22, 1971, and was tortured and denied sleep for a week. Another example is Yang Chin-hai, who also was severely tortured. They stripped him and made him crawl about the floor. I think the purpose of this kind of torture is to completely strip a person of any human dignity. Still a third example is Wang Hsing-nan, who was kidnapped by the KMT from Hong Kong and brought back to Taiwan. The KMT sent him to the hospital. Do you know how much his medical expenses were? U.S.$5,000. So you can see how badly he was beaten. There are many other examples; I simply do not have time to mention them all.

We Taiwanese pay taxes; we serve in the armed forces; we fulfill every obligation of citizens. But what rights do we have? We cannot elect the government, and we do not enjoy any kind of human rights at all. In addition, this government has led Taiwan to complete isolation in the international community. The government was kicked out of the United Nations and could not attend the Olympics. At the present time, only about 20 countries recognize Taiwan.

I believe that from both the Chinese point of view and the Taiwanese point of view there is no justification for this regime's existence.

George: I may be mistaken, but I have the impression you are saying that Chinese are foreigners. I wonder if you could clarify for me whether those of us who were not born in Taiwan are foreigners. What about people such as my son, who was born in Taiwan and has gone through schooling there. Is he also a foreigner? Are you Chinese?

Lawrence: I am not Chinese. We Taiwanese have been in Taiwan for 300 years. We have never been in China. It is a completely strange land to us. I do not have any emotional attachment to that land at all. I do not think I am Chinese just as Americans do not think they are British—they are American.

If your son thinks he is Taiwanese, then of course he is Taiwanese. At dinner Albert said that although he was born in China, he thinks he is an American psychologically. The same applies to your son.

George: But he thinks he is Chinese also.

Lawrence: If he thinks he is Chinese and wants to go to the Mainland, he can do that. But if he wants to stay in Taiwan, he would be welcome.

The essence of the Taiwan independence movement is that the people on Taiwan who do not like the Communists must face the reality that it is impossible to recover the Mainland. The consequence of this fact is that we must establish our own country on Taiwan; otherwise China would have an excuse to attack, or to "liberate" Taiwan.

All the people in Taiwan, whether they were born in Taiwan or came from the Chinese mainland, should get together and establish a government of their own, if they think that Taiwan is the place where they will be living.

David: I do not think there should be a distinction drawn between Taiwanese and Mainlanders. Years ago it was possible to tell a Taiwanese from a Mainlander, in part by how one spoke. But now, it is very hard to tell people apart. There have also been a lot of intermarriages. I want to stress the idea of equal opportunity. People born in Taiwan and even people who have only been there a few months should be considered equal residents of the area.

Frank: I wonder whether we are getting into a definitional problem about the term "Chinese." You can regard a person as Chinese on the basis of political loyalty or ethnic origin or cultural identity. Many people in Singapore are politically Singaporean citizens, but are ethnically Chinese. There are Italian-Americans who are Italian by origin, but full-fledged Americans in terms of political loyalty.

My personal view is that if you go to Taiwan and ask the majority of people whether they are Chinese or Taiwanese, they would answer that they are both. They are Taiwanese because of history and other factors, but they are also Chinese by ethnic origin.

A. ". . . workers in Taiwan are doing quite well."

Matthew: In your statistics, Lawrence, you speak of 100 percent of this and 100 percent of that being Chinese. Suppose those people tell you that they identify their futures and their lives with Taiwan. From what you said, we should regard them as Taiwanese. But in your statistics you still seem to count them as non-Taiwanese.

You also stress that the Taiwanese have been deprived of political participation. You forget that after 1949 virtually all the people on both sides of the Taiwan Strait have been denied participation. It's not just one part of the population; it's the whole population.

Some of your logic bothers me. You mentioned that Wang Yung-ching got rich from the poor people and that this violates the principle of People's Livelihood. Frankly, I do not understand this. Restricting capital does not mean making everybody poor, or prohibiting anybody from getting rich. In fact, with regard to differences between the rich and the poor, Taiwan probably has a better record than any Asian country today.[2]

As for wages, it is true that strikes are not allowed, but the market situation determines that the wages must rise. This year the wages are about 50 percent higher than last year.[3] The free market will make these adjustments by itself. Frankly, I do not think that your logic would convince people.

---

2   According to Taiwan government figures, the family income of the top 20 percent of earners was only 4.18 times higher than the bottom 20 percent in 1976. Council for Economic Planning and Development, Taiwan Statistical Data Book 1978, at 53.

3   Contrast the Taiwan government figures for annual increase in per capita income showing increases of 8.1,-2.2, 0.2, 9.6, and 5.9 percent for the years 1972-76, respectively. *Id.* at 30.

Lawrence: Sun Yat-sen's principle of restriction of capital was to prevent the accumulation of a great deal of capital in the hands of a small number of people. It also favors equal distribution of national wealth and national income. Has the government made any policies to prevent concentration of capital or to prevent the unequal distribution of national wealth and national income? If the government had done that, then Wang could not have become a billionaire in such a short period of time.

Matthew: That logic still bothers me.

Stephen: I think that both the Taiwan independence movement and the PRC greatly overemphasize poverty on Taiwan and greatly underemphasize the important economic progress that has been made there. If you are talking about rising living standards, I think workers in Taiwan are doing quite well. Both the independence people and the PRC downplay that fact. The independence movement is not merely a function of economics, and that aspect of it can be exaggerated.

B. *"The [American] Pledge of Allegiance says '. . . one nation, . . . indivisible . . . .' "*

Albert: Lawrence's comments have centered on the fact that the KMT is a very bad government. Although it may be possible to overthrow a bad government, it does not necessarily follow that an independent Taiwan state could be created. Could you give me a reason, other than the fact that this is a bad government, that gives you the right to declare an independent state?

Lawrence: Taiwan belongs to the Taiwanese. The principle of self-determination should be applied. The 17 million people on Taiwan should be free to establish a new nation, independent from China, representing all the people in Taiwan.

William: I am not certain that either morality or politics unambiguously requires that one should always support the principle of self-determination.

The United States fought a civil war in part over the issue of whether one piece of the country could break off to form a separate country. The Pledge of Allegiance says ". . . one nation, . . . indivisible . . . ." If America is indivisible, then we must explain why the Chinese case is different. When the issue is Namibia, everyone agrees that self-determination should apply. But what about Quebec,

Puerto Rico, Kurdistan, Free Lebanon, South Molucca, or the PLO? We have no clear moral principle on how to view the question of self-determination.

In addition, even if there were a moral obligation to get the consent of the 17 million people on Taiwan, this obligation would run into considerations of power politics. At this point, I think the United States does not know how to strike a balance between considerations of morality and of power politics.

As a practical matter, I also think that merely appealing to the morality of this situation would not be effective in the United States, or, I suspect, in Japan. And without support from these two countries, the effort to bring about self-determination is not going to work.

C. *"But look at the results in Iran. Is that what you expect to happen in Taiwan?"*

Lawrence: How can independence be achieved? I strongly believe that the will and determination of the people on Taiwan will prevail. We have already struggled for many years. The movement first started overseas, with only a small number of Formosans participating. Gradually, especially in recent times, almost all Formosans outside of Taiwan support independence in one way or another.

I can give you some specific examples. Hsu Hsin-liang was educated in England and brought the idea of Taiwan independence back to Taiwan. Chang Chun-hung came to the United States a few years ago. At that time he was a KMT member, but after returning to Taiwan he abandoned the KMT and strongly advocated Taiwan independence. About five years ago he ran for city councilman in Taipei. He printed 100,000 flyers in which he said that he was a political doctor and would cure the political problems in Taiwan. How to cure these problems? By declaring Taiwan a sovereign independent nation.

Lu Hsiu-lien has been in the United States for many years. After returning to Taiwan, she denounced the KMT and worked for Taiwan independence; still another example is Lin I-hsiung.*

This kind of support from abroad has an effect on our brothers and sisters in Taiwan. The reaction of the masses has been very positive: Look at the Chungli uprising and Hsu's birthday party.

*These descriptions are disputed by others. See William's comment on page 59.

These are very good starts. If the present situation continues, as I expect it to, the KMT will have to use armed force to control the situation. As you know, more than 80 percent of the soldiers are Taiwanese. When the officers ask these soldiers to fire upon the people of Taiwan, I really doubt that the soldiers will comply. They will refuse to take orders from the officers.

You can see the situation in Iran. When soldiers refused to take orders from the officers, the officers had no choice but to run away. In Iran there were demonstrations for three or four months before the government was overthrown. In Taiwan, the government will be overthrown in the early stages of a demonstration.

I strongly believe this is the right way to go. In the near future we can achieve this goal.

George: But look at the results in Iran. Is that what you expect to happen in Taiwan? Khomeini launched a large-scale purge to get rid of his political opponents. If the Nationalists are overthrown, will there be a sweeping political purge and large-scale political persecution?

Lawrence: It appears that we have only that alternative. Of course we will try to avoid violence if possible, but to avoid violence the KMT also must take some actions: first, declare Taiwan a new and independent country; second, call for a new island-wide election for all elective offices in the central government; third, lift martial law and respect fundamental human rights such as freedom of speech and freedom of association; fourth, release all political prisoners.

If the KMT is willing to do these things, then perhaps we can achieve self-determination and independence through peaceful means. But I doubt very much that the KMT will do so.

William: Are you saying that if the KMT does not take these steps, then there will be a purge of the KMT after independence?

Lawrence: Of course. But let me clarify one point. The purpose of the independence movement is to broaden political participation in Taiwan. After the Chiang Kai-shek government is overthrown, the people in Taiwan, whether Taiwanese or Chinese, will have equal rights to participate in the government. What we are opposed to is a very small KMT elite ruling the island. Actually, the majority of Chinese oppose the Chiang Kai-shek regime as much as we do.

Vincent: I am glad you put your position so forcefully. That is what we need in our discussions. I know that some unexpected things do happen, so I do not exclude any possibility. We have to keep in mind the possibility of a new independent nation of Taiwan.

However, I am troubled by a number of points. I believe that your historical statement that Taiwan has not been part of China since 1895 is true but one-sided. For 50 years it was part of the Japanese empire, but many Chinese and some Taiwanese regarded the separation as an unfortunate situation imposed upon China. The fact of being separated from China should not be seen in isolation from these other feelings.

It is also true that Taiwan has not been a part of China for the last 30 years. But I do not think you can convince the majority of people in the PRC or the KMT that this is a strong argument for asserting that Taiwan should not be part of China. These people see the separation as an unfortunate consequence of the civil war between the Communists and the Nationalists.

What I am saying is that for people who are not already ideologically convinced of your position, the statement that the KMT represents no one is hyperbolic. It is a campaign speech; it is not factual.

We also must be aware that if independence occurs there are several things that almost certainly will happen. First, there will be a sizeable minority of people on Taiwan, call them KMT if you like, who will resist independence. If you grant my premise, which you may not, that the KMT represents somebody, then there will be people in Taiwan who will not be happy when a new government comes in. Second, for some indefinite number of years the PRC will not accept Taiwan's independence. That has been stated by the PRC many times.

I am not saying that just because there may be bad consequences following the establishment of a new nation of Taiwan, the step should not be taken. I am merely pointing out that we should recognize all the consequences of this action.

I resist your line of reasoning which says that right now the situation is intolerable, and that the establishment of a new government would be the beginning of the solution of the problem. I do not think that the problem will go away with the creation of a new government.

D. *". . . suppose there is a really fair and free election in which Chiang Ching-kuo is elected."*

Stephen: Lawrence has presented very clearly and forcefully the conditions he thinks must be met to prevent a revolution in Taiwan. Let me ask: Suppose in the next year the KMT meets some of these conditions? For example, if it agrees to hold an election for all the seats in the Legislature, the National Assembly and the Control Yuan, and even have popular election of the president. And suppose Chiang Ching-kuo runs for president and is elected. Would the independence movement support the results of a relatively fair and free election in which Chiang Ching-kuo won?

Lawrence: Fair and free? We should have freedom of speech so that we can discuss any issue we like. We should also be allowed to form a political party to compete fairly with the KMT. I doubt very much the KMT will accept that.

Stephen: But suppose the KMT does? I think that a politician, when faced with the prospect of total defeat, will tend to compromise. At this stage, the KMT is trying to think of some ways to cope with the current situation. It is ready to make some compromises. Your list of demands may not be entirely acceptable to the KMT, but I think it will make some kind of concessions in order to stay in power.

Again, suppose there is a really fair and free election in which Chiang Ching-kuo is elected. Will you fight the result, or will you say that your conditions have been met?

Lawrence: This is a purely hypothetical and academic question. You know the KMT much better than I do. Do you think the KMT will allow a free election? In the past 30 years there have been elections. But you can campaign for only ten days and have only five or six campaign workers. You cannot criticize governmental policy or the KMT.

Stephen: But look at the 1977 election. The fact that a number of non-KMT candidates were elected indicates that there is some degree of freedom. I think the degree of freeness and fairness will increase as the years go by.

Lawrence: At a minimum we want freedom of assembly and the right to form an opposition party. We also need freedom of speech so that anything can be discussed, including attacks on the KMT and Chiang Ching-kuo's leadership. If the regime can meet these conditions, we will accept the results.

Henry: I am not so sure that the present government in Taiwan will be willing to take the kind of actions you describe. Judging from recent events such as the Yu and Hsu cases,[4] I do not think that the KMT is sincere about broadening political participation.

If anyone in this room can guarantee that there will be greater participation by local people, my own viewpoint is that people will accept the KMT actions; but no one here can guarantee that.

The people on that island have only one request and that is for much, much greater political participation.   If the situation in Taiwan does not change, then I think the consequences will be very unfavorable.

E. *". . . the United States derives no benefit from an independent Taiwan."*

Albert: I came here very interested in hearing Lawrence's presentation because I wanted to hear the position of the independence movement. But I am very disappointed. You provide no arguments whatsoever. You have no factual basis whatsoever. You mention two or three names. They mean nothing to me; the data are statistically insignificant.

Some of the other points have been mentioned before.   The principle of self-determination is not universally accepted by the international community.   From the American point of view, the United States derives no benefit from an independent Taiwan. Independence would disrupt the entire balance of power, stability, and business interests of the United States. I feel very strongly that if there is any kind of disruption in Taiwan, American companies will pull out. Without American companies Taiwan cannot be prosperous.

Moreover, you are already making threats of retaliation against the KMT. This is definitely against American principles; Americans will not tolerate any kind of terrorist or lawless situation. Look at Iran today; the American public is 100 percent against Iran.

---

4   Hsu Hsin-liang was suspended for two years from his elected office as magistrate of Tao-yuan county in May 1979 for allegedly violating a law prohibiting elected officials from participating in other people's election campaigns.

I think your task is to present a more credible argument before we can consider your position more seriously. How would independence benefit the Taiwanese people? How would it benefit the international community? How would it benefit the United States? Without answers to these questions I would consider your position a lost cause; I would not even consider it an option.

Lawrence: Whether Taiwan independence serves the interests of the Taiwanese people is a factual issue. A plebiscite can determine who is right.

My own belief is that the people of Taiwan have the right to determine their own future. In addition, the independence of Taiwan will serve international peace and security in the Pacific.

Albert: How? The PRC will attack Taiwan. The Chinese have made very clear that one of the conditions under which nonpeaceful means may be used is the declaration of an independent Taiwan.

Lawrence: So long as the KMT continues to exist in Taiwan, China will want to destroy this regime, which challenges the PRC's legitimacy. China might even use the KMT's oppression of the people as an excuse to "liberate" the Taiwanese. By removing the KMT, we can prevent the Chinese civil war from coming to Taiwan.

You also ask whether the independence will serve the interests of the United States. That is not my concern. Still, I would say that American and Japanese interests would be served. Much of Japanese shipping goes near the Taiwan region. If China attacks or takes over Taiwan and the relations between China and Japan become worse as a result, China could blockade the area. In one week the economy of Japan would collapse. Japan needs oil and raw materials from the Middle East and from Southeast Asia.

The United States is committed to defend Japan's supply lines. If there is a blockade, the United States would have to send in military forces. So if Taiwan falls into the hands of China, the chances of military conflict between China and the United States would increase rather than decrease. But if Taiwan becomes an independent country, it will not blockade Japanese shipping.

Vincent: I can see that from Lawrence's point of view independence will serve the interests of the Taiwanese people. But I want to repeat that the PRC is likely to try even more strongly to retake Taiwan if Taiwan becomes independent. The PRC may not succeed, but I take its warnings very seriously.

William: I agree that we should take seriously the PRC statements about taking action. The PRC position is based not only on the grounds of nationalism or the greater China syndrome, but also on domestic political factors. A leader in Peking, whether pragmatic or radical, must react strenuously to independence; otherwise, he cannot face his constituents.

Just for the record, let me add that I think Hsu Hsin-liang and the other opposition leaders Lawrence mentioned would be quite surprised and displeased by his statement that they advocate Taiwan independence.

> F. *"I really do not like the Taiwan independence movement. It is destructive and not constructive."*

Vincent: Let me try to be intentionally provocative. I realize that the people in the independence movement are fully committed to the idea of independence. But many of us do not assume *ipso facto* that the independence of Taiwan is a good thing. Our feelings are conditional. If the KMT goes down the wrong path and increases suppression— and let us not kid ourselves, the KMT has a bad record—then your argument would gain in persuasiveness. But what if the KMT moves the other way? I suggest that if the ROC makes genuine reforms and allows full political participation, then the Taiwan independence movement should give up its effort to establish an independent Taiwan. In addition to achieving reforms, this approach may ease Taiwan's relations with the PRC. If the ROC could be reassured that the Taiwan independence movement has lost its steam, then I think a great deal of the KMT's fears would be removed and it will become more flexible.

George: As I see it, Taiwan is most concerned at this point not with what Peking might do, but with the secessionist movement, that is, the Taiwan independence movement.

I really do not like this movement. It is destructive and not constructive. What the Taiwan people really want today is not a new group of leaders; what the people really want is reform, real, tangible, substantive reform. They want greater political participation, but not a participation based on a narrow-minded parochialism that says one set of people is Taiwanese and the others are outsiders.

If we address ourselves to the Taiwan problem in such a narrow manner, there will be no future. The Taiwan independence movement adherents may have strong emotions, but they will arrive at a dead end. I think a lot of people both in and out of the government will resist them. The movement's members may have a commitment, but these other people also have their commitment.

Peking may use the secessionist movement or Taiwan independence as part of the united front effort, but in fact Peking does not agree with it either.

Let me tell you what the real feeling is. On Taiwan today the greatest discrimination is being carried out by Taiwanese. This is a fact. I visited a number of large corporations where the leadership contained not a single non-Taiwanese. I visited factories where there was not a single non-Taiwanese employee.

What kind of political and economic system will you establish if you take over? If tomorrow all the Nationalists dropped dead and the leaders of the Taiwan independence movement were installed in the government, what would you do? I have not heard any adequate description of what the new government will look like. Whenever we try to have a discussion about this, the conversation deteriorates into bitter and unfortunate polemics. If you keep up your rigidity and escalate your rhetoric, you lose the chance for a rational exchange of views.

Lawrence: You say that the political situation in Taiwan is so good. You mention elections, but these are only local elections. If Taiwan is to become a model for the Chinese mainland, how do you explain the fact that martial law has been imposed on Taiwan since 1948?

You also say that the primary concern of the Taiwan regime is the Taiwan independence movement, and that you resent this movement. I can understand that, because when people stand up, a minority regime loses all its political power, like the white minority regimes in Rhodesia and South Africa.

Henry: I would like to ask George a question. You said that the primary fear of the ROC is not the PRC, but rather the secessionist movement. You also said that this movement is a dead-end effort. These two statements seem contradictory to me.

George: I have traveled widely and talked to many people in Taiwan—factory workers, students, technocrats, and so forth. They are concerned with things like marriage and jobs, not with independence.

Many of us have the chance to travel in Taiwan. We should ask about Taiwan independence. People will give you straightforward answers; don't be fooled about that. It was said earlier that 90 percent of the people support independence. I think that estimate is exaggerated and unfounded.

At the present time the Nationalist government is not particularly worried about military attack from the PRC. On the other hand, it is worried about the secessionist movement working in combination with the united front organizations in Peking to create disturbance in Taiwan. I say the movement is at a dead end because it does not have public support.

Henry: If that is the case, you should not be afraid of the independence movement; you should just forget about it.

George: I did not say that the ROC was fearful, only concerned and worried. So far, I think that the KMT has used considerable restraint in handling this problem and has avoided the use of force.

James: I doubt that the ROC's principal concern at this time is the Taiwan independence movement. As I see it, some of the people in the KMT may want to use the independence movement as a whipping boy in order to show the PRC that there is a basis for cooperation between the PRC and the ROC. This gives an inducement to the PRC to adopt a moderate approach to the Taiwan problem in order not to alienate the KMT leadership.

G. ". . . the tyranny of the minority will be transformed into the tyranny of the majority."

Edward: I am pleased that George raised the issue of the mutual perceptions of prejudice and discrimination. I share some of his sentiments about discrimination against mainland Chinese.

For the last 30 years, Taiwan has been, in the terms of the Kerner Commission report, one country but two nations. Taiwanese and Mainlanders mutually dislike each other. They feel hatred, prejudice, and mistrust—a lot of mistrust. This in turn has led to mutual discrimination.

As we have seen in the public sector, the Mainlanders have a virtual monopoly of the higher-ranking positions. This is true in the government, the army, the security apparatus, the major intellectual institutions, and the publicly-owned enterprises.

If you look at the economic structure, more than 50 percent of Taiwan's capital assets are in the public sector. The government inherited those assets and corporations left over by the Japanese, which it then expanded and further developed.

The Mainlanders have used this public sector to create a welfare bureaucracy for themselves. This development in the early 1950s solved the very important problem of how to provide jobs for those Mainlanders who came to Taiwan. But in the ensuing years, the welfare bureaucracy for the Mainlanders has become institutiona- lized. Few Taiwanese have been promoted or have hope of being promoted to high positions in the public sector, regardless of their qualifications or competence.

But in the private sector, the Taiwanese discriminate against the mainland Chinese. A mainland Chinese youth graduating from high school or college has virtually no chance of getting into an operation run by Taiwanese. Even if he is lucky enough to get in, his chances of moving up are not as good as those of a Taiwanese. This is just the reverse of the situation in the public sector.

Thus what we have here is a vicious circle of mutual discrimina- tion. The Mainlanders are discriminated against in the private sector, and the native Taiwanese are discriminated against in the public sector.

A lot of mainland Chinese now follow the KMT political line, but not because they genuinely believe in some of that nonsense. I would say that more than 90 percent of the Mainlanders, that is everyone except the very old, know that there is no chance of returning to the Mainland. Why do they accept the KMT and reject any other alternative? Because of fear—fear that if the Taiwanese take over, the tyranny of the minority may be transformed into the tyranny of the majority. Even if some mainland Chinese may not favor a tyranny of the minority, they still tolerate the present arrangement because of the benefits they derive. But if a tyranny of the majority develops, the mainland Chinese will lose their special privileges and perogatives. Thus they see themselves as the net losers in the democratization process.

For this reason, the KMT continues to find its support among the mainland Chinese. To perpetuate its one-party rule, the KMT exploits the unstated but genuine fears and mistrust between the native Taiwanese and mainlander Chinese. It tries to prevent the political activists of the two groups from ever joining forces to present a viable political alternative. When necessary, it has not hesitated to resort to outright ruthless suppression. The late Lei Chen, the respected liberal journalist and statesman from mainland China, tried to join forces with the native Taiwanese elite of the same persuasion.[5] We all know what happened to him—thrown into jail for ten years on a fabricated charge.

In the 15 years since the Lei Chen affair, the KMT has succeeded at preventing any attempts in collaboration between the political activists of the two groups. However, the ice was broken a few years ago. I attach great significance to the fact that Lin Cheng-chieh, a college student born on Taiwan of Mainlander parentage, campaigned vigorously for Hsu Hsin-liang, one of the most promising and charismatic of the new generation of the native political activists. More recently, another Mainlander intellectual, Chen Ku-ying,[6] worked with the native political activists in the December 1978 election campaign, as well as in the subsequent protest movement. Perhaps this is the beginning of a new era. As a matter of principle, I wish to see more collaboration between native Taiwanese and mainlander Chinese. To facilitate this healthy trend, the new generation of young political activists must squarely face the problem of the psychological and political schism between the Taiwan majority and Mainlander minority. They also must address the unstated but genuine fear on the part of many Mainlanders regarding the consequences of drastic change in the political status quo. They must assure the Mainlanders, by words and by deeds, that democratization will serve the best interests of *everyone* on the island. This is a difficult but not impossible task. Sweeping the issue of mutual distrust and fear under the rug as if it does not exist is merely playing into the hands of the KMT.

George: I talked with someone on Taiwan and I was shocked at what he said. He put it bluntly: "The Taiwan independence people are so parochial and narrow-minded; they talk about discrimination and prejudice, but once they take power there will be no future for people from the Mainland. The independence people have no compassion. We have no land; we have no money. Where will we go if the Taiwanese take over?"

---

5 On Lei Chen, see Wen Te, *Lei Chen, Hu Shih, and the KMT: A Chapter in the History of the Taiwan Democratization Movement and a Memorial to Lei Chen,* Pa-shih nien-tai [The Eighties], vol. 1, no. 3, pp. 87-89 (Aug. 1979).

6 For his political views, see Chen Ku-ying, *Min-chu kuang-ch'ang* [Democracy Forum] (Taipei 1978).

If the Nationalists are pushed too far, they may prefer to work out a secret deal with the PRC rather than let the island become independent. I am not saying that this is the government's official position; all I am saying is that some people think this way.

I have had some contact with Taiwan independence movement leaders. They talk a lot about political oppression, but there is also another kind of oppression, a subtle one: economic oppression.

Vincent: I have to jump in here. I understand your sentiment, but the bald fact is that the KMT is in power. I am not terribly persuaded when you say that the economic discrimination exercised by the Taiwanese against the Mainlanders is equivalent to the political discrimination the Mainlanders exercise against the Taiwanese.

It may be that if the Taiwan independence movement takes power, these people may be even more oppressive, but that has not happened yet.

I have spoken earlier about my feelings regarding the Taiwan independence movement. I am against it. But I am also not persuaded by the people who have been talking to you. Economic discrimination cannot be equated with political discrimination.

Henry: I keep hearing George saying derogatory things about the Taiwan independence movement. You must realize that, like it or not, the Taiwanese make up 85 percent of the population. I am not saying that the majority must oppress the minority. But unfortunately the situation there is just the reverse. What else is there to say?

But instead of acknowledging that position, you keep attacking the Taiwan independence movement. I come from Taiwan, and I have a strong sentimental attachment to my home country, too.

George: This was not an attack. It was a statement of fact, as I have experienced and observed.

V

Change on Taiwan,
Internal and External

Albert: *I do not think we should be telling Taiwan what percent of the National Legislature should be locally elected. After all, we are not citizens of Taiwan. We do not pay taxes there. We do not have the right to tell Taiwan what to do. I think Taiwan would resent it, and it is also unfair.*

Frank: I think we are moving toward a partial consensus about the situation in Taiwan. There *are* problems there—some feel a sense of injustice, others worry about the presence of people who are concerned primarily with the maintenance of their power.

The radical Taiwan independence group and the conservative KMT group have been launching charges and countercharges for 30 years. It is time to look at how these problems can be defused and also to examine what are their real causes. We have to deal with the more practical question of what can be done.

If nothing is done, I think we do have a second consensus that something very abrupt and disruptive may happen. Politics is a very passionate thing; that has been evident here at our meeting. My own belief is that neither extreme—doing nothing or violently overthrowing the government—is going to promote the interests of peace and well-being.

William: Let me ask a question to help me focus on the issue of what can be done. How much change must occur to satisfy those who are presently dissatisfied with the government, without going so far as to provoke a severe reaction from the conservative wing of the KMT?

For example, is Hungdah Chiu's article in *Chung-kuo shih-pao* part of the mainstream of current political thought, or does it tilt toward the left or the right? As I understand it, the thrust of his proposal is that there should be a new election for approximately 50 percent of the National Assembly, Legislature, and Control Yuan.[1] The other half of the seats will be either appointed by the President or retained by the incumbents. The rationale is that the reality of the 17 million people on Taiwan is accommodated by allowing them to elect a substantial proportion of the officials. At the same time, the ideological claim of representing the Mainland justifies the appointment of the other half of the officeholders—and in that way assures that the KMT will remain in control.

Albert: What is the legal basis for being able to make this change?

William: These three bodies have the power to determine or define their own membership. The Legislature may have to amend some of the laws, but in any case, the Legislature and the President acting together can certainly make these changes.

Albert: I think it would be ludicrous to change the political structure in this way. Those assemblies were meant to be representative of all of China. If there is going to be a change, I say we should abolish all of these national offices. The President should establish some kind of emergency ad hoc legislative council, all of whose members should be elected by the Taiwan people.

Vincent: You are asking the KMT to commit political suicide.

Albert: No, the KMT will not be committing political suicide; it will still be the majority party. I just think it should stop basing itself on a body that claims to represent all of China.

I am not necessarily in favor of a totally new election. All I am saying is that if the proposal is to elect half and appoint half, we may be better off reelecting the entire body or creating a new ad hoc agency. You cannot have a government representing all of China that has half its membership elected only by the local people on Taiwan.

---

1   Hungdah Chiu, *Certain Questions Relating to the Maintenance of the International Status of the ROC,* Chung-kuo shih-pao [China Times], Apr. 27, 1979 (in Chinese). A similar proposal was recently made by Kang Ning-hsiang, Huang Hsin-chieh, and Fei Hsi-ping (opposition members of the National Legislature), *Discussion on Reforming Central Representative Organs,* Hua-ch'iao jih-pao [Overseas Chinese Daily], Oct. 1, 1979 (in Chinese).

Let me make some suggestions. The only thing that makes sense is for the current government to respond to the needs of Taiwan by immediately stopping the pretense of being all of China. This can be done without changing any of the national titles; there will still be a government.

Second, the President, if he has the legal authority, should establish an ad hoc council to be elected by the people on Taiwan, with perhaps some representation from the Chinatowns of New York and San Francisco.

William: Could you respond to Vincent's comment that this may be an act of political suicide? If an election were held in Taiwan for all these offices, how could the KMT be assured that it would be able to maintain control?

Albert: I would assume that the KMT could win many seats in the election. As I recall, there are about 1.5 million KMT members, including many native Taiwanese. In terms of the general membership of the party, the proportion of native Taiwanese is very high. Seventy percent of the party membership is Taiwanese, although these members do not hold many of the higher offices.

Obviously these people hold some position in society, and I assume that they will win elections.

A. *"Without systematic reform on Taiwan, I think the leadership is sitting on top of a volcano that will explode."*

Matthew: The Chiu article is one of a series of proposals for reform; but they all run into one serious difficulty. They do not deal with the issue of constitutional rigidity. The problem being faced by the central committee working group is how to twist or extend the constitution to make such changes possible. I tried to tell a member of that group that they are looking for a solution when they know there is none. In doing so, they are losing time, and people are getting impatient.

The impatience of the opposition leaders and followers is already very visible. It will soon reach a level of intolerance. That would be very dangerous—not only to the orderly progress of society, but also to the development of the opposition forces. The opposition has not had the time to gain experience and develop. I once told Kang Ning-hsiang that the opposition movement is like a fried doughnut [*yu-t'iao*]; when you throw it in hot oil it puffs up to a great size, but there is no content inside. If the opposition would take a little more time, it could build a more solid base, as well as develop a second echelon of leaders.

Actually, the KMT need not be very worried about committing political suicide through a broad election. My estimate is that the KMT can win about 60 percent of the seats. The KMT did recruit and groom quite a few capable people; we cannot just wipe out all these good people. For instance, the new governor of Taiwan is quite capable. Such a person will automatically win support with or without KMT backing. If the KMT relies on these people, it really is not committing suicide.

I would suggest that the KMT take a dramatic and seemingly drastic step to find a solution to the constitutional problem. It should allow a direct referendum to determine what changes should be made. This step would maintain a smooth transition, so that the overall progress on the island would not be disrupted. With the full participation of the people in this new kind of arrangement, the government would be able to command not only respect, but also wholehearted support. In that case, it would be able to negotiate new terms for relationships with other governments as well as with the other side of the strait.

This approach also would enable the new generation to gradually take over the entire responsibility. The inevitable results would be localization of the power structure, and even relinquishment of the claims that the ROC is the government of all of China and will return to the Mainland. We all know that these have been myths anyway.

So, to me, this step would not be political suicide, but rather a lifesaving procedure leading to the modernization of the political structure.

Frank: I want to underline a point that has come up several times already. Without systematic reform on Taiwan, I think the leadership is sitting on top of a volcano that will explode. With or without reform, I think political change will occur. From my point of view, I would like to see a peaceful transition rather than an explosive situation that sacrifices lives and property.

Edward: The various political forces in Taiwan have a kind of symbiotic relationship. None can survive without the others. They will live together or perish together. Taiwan is a ticking time bomb that may explode at any moment in the next few years. In view of what happened in the last few years, I feel that it is no exaggeration to say that the explosion may occur in the near future unless there is an alleviation of tensions. How do we defuse the time bomb? I consider a 50 percent election a first step toward eventual meaningful reform. There should also be a rule that anyone who reaches the age of 65 or 70 must retire. If this process continues for 10 or 15 years, the Legislature will become a body that is elected locally and is responsible to local constituencies. This will lead to genuine political participation.

Even now the Legislature does not make law. Power resides in the Executive Yuan, which is responsible to the President, and in the Central Committee of the KMT.

The reason the Legislature has not been able to carry out its constitutional functions is that the legislators do not have local constituencies. But once the Legislature is elected locally, the KMT will not be able to order it to do this or that. The members would have to respond to their local constituencies who elected them, and not to the KMT. This in turn would lead to a viable two-party or multi-party system, and would really democratize the decision-making structure.

Philip: During the election campaign last December, some opposition people calculated the death rate for members of the National Assembly and Legislature combined.[2] One member will die every week in the years ahead. Some of the KMT leaders obviously feel that this natural rate of elimination was bad enough for the Mainlander old guard. Eventually, most or all of the members of these bodies will be elected locally. Why rush things prematurely!

William: I saw the actuarial chart. As I recall, after ten years half will have died, and after 30 years all of them. It makes a real difference how much of the leadership would be replaced after five or ten years.

B. ". . . the inevitable result of genuine democratization will be an end to one-party rule and a move toward independence . . . ."

Edward: The KMT has said it is committed to further democratization, but has done everything possible to thwart its growth. Why? I suspect that the diehards in the top echelon of the party feel that the

---

2   *1978 Taiwan tang-wai ching-hsuan ch'uan-tan chi* [Collection of 1978 Elections Materials of the Non-party Candidates in Taiwan] 61 (published by Taiwan shu-wu, address unknown 1978).

inevitable result of genuine democratization will be an end to one-party rule and a move toward independence, either de jure or de facto. The two developments are intertwined and tend to reinforce each other.

I suspect the PRC leadership has been always aware of this delicate dynamic. Its support for the political reform movement in Taiwan has been half-hearted, except where it sees an opportunity to exploit the situation to its own advantage, such as in the case of Yu Teng-fa. It feels that it has a better chance of liberating Taiwan, peacefully or otherwise, with the KMT in firm control. The task will be much more difficult should the native Taiwanese come to share or take over decision-making power. This explains why Peking has continued to appeal to the KMT top brass for a negotiated settlement and has virtually ignored the protestations of the Taiwanese that they be a party to any negotiations. In other words, I suspect that Peking is more wary of the native Taiwanese political reformers than the KMT. As long as the mainlander KMT elite monopolizes political power, there is a prospect, however dim, of a negotiated settlement on terms favorable to Peking. But if the KMT does not allow this process of democratization to develop, then, as someone else put it, it is sitting on a volcano. The choice facing the KMT is very hard.

It seems to me that the problem is not structural change, although there will, of course, be structural change. In the last analysis, the problem is the great China syndrome. The Chinese do not seem able to make a distinction between cultural identification as a Chinese and political identification with a particular state. This psychological hang-up afflicts Chinese on both sides of the strait.

Many of the younger generation are willing to make a clean sweep of the past and make the distinction between cultural and political identity. But I wonder whether the same change of attitude is taking place among the middle-aged and older Chinese.

Matthew: I can only give you my own impression. Among the top leaders of the KMT, the conservatives form a majority. They will gradually die out, but currently they simply cannot accept the reality of their situation.

Many of the persons just entering the top leadership are young, and many are Taiwan-born or native Taiwanese. The Mainlanders under 50 years of age overwhelmingly prefer localization of the political process. They do not see their futures tied to mainland China. Their careers and their futures are right there on Taiwan.

I think the key issue is localization. If this grows, the PRC can see that Taiwan would not make any claim beyond the territory under its actual control. In that case, Taiwan's challenge to the Mainland's position would already have disappeared.

Let me add that the idea of electing 50 percent new members in the Legislature creates a new problem. Under this proposal, the number of voters needed to elect a member of the national legislature would be less than the number needed to elect a member of the provincial legislature. So solving one problem creates another.

Vincent: I would urge a sweeping new election. At a minimum, the election that would have taken place in December, if Carter had not stupidly jumped the gun, should be resumed as quickly as possible. I hope that a good many Taiwanese will obtain positions. After that we can look to the next election.

I am willing to accept Chiu's 50 percent formula or any similar formula. But we must realize that these are stop-gap measures. If we are talking about sweeping change, then we would need a completely new election.

Frank: Let me try to summarize where I think we are. There is a broad consensus, although not unanimous, that the most serious problem in Taiwan concerns the need to share power and broaden political participation. On the economic side there may be some problems, but nothing of crisis proportions.

The arguments concerning the extreme positions of reunification and Taiwan independence are quite clear. It is the middle range of gradual to drastic change that is more confusing. As I see it, there are a number of possibilities here. The most drastic step, but still less than outright independence, is to change the entire constitutional structure and carry out a plebiscite to determine the future of Taiwan. Next would be preserving the present constitutional framework but amending certain aspects, particularly those dealing with the election of central level bodies. The proposals range from a totally new election to a 75 or 50 percent change. The third position is simply to resume the election suspended last December. In addition, the number of seats to be elected might be increased slightly. The final possibility is to take no action, on the ground that because of the present dangerous position the election of last December should remain suspended.

David: I look at these things in a different way. Politicians always say they want to serve the people, but I think sometimes they forget about the people and do them a disservice. From my very naive viewpoint, I do not think it is possible to have democracy unless there is more than one political party. An individual or small group just does not have the power to fight an entire party. Both Peking and Taipei talk about democracy, but they will arrest anyone who disagrees with them. I do not know whether the Communists have two parties, but I doubt it. The KMT talk about three parties, but two of the parties are very weak.

I do not know why the Chinese cannot have two parties like other people. Maybe we need the Taiwan Strait to separate the Communist Party and the Nationalist Party. When you put the two in one room, they start fighting.

It also seems to me that many high-ranking KMT leaders are out of touch. Recently in Washington, D.C., one such person made a speech in which he said that when the KMT came to Taiwan the island was poor and backward. The KMT, he said, had to do so much to help develop Taiwan. That claim is nonsense, and it also hurts people's feelings.

I was seven years old when the Chinese came to Taiwan in 1945. At that time Taiwan had a railroad from Keelung to Kaoshiung, cement factories, and many other things. Very few provinces in China were up to the standard of Taiwan, except perhaps Kiangsu Province and some of the Japanese-controlled areas in Manchuria. The KMT should not have the attitude that "We helped you so much, you should always show appreciation to us."

I see many different points of view here, but I think we all agree on one thing. We would like to avoid violence or war if possible. No one wants to see people killed. We have talked about alternatives if peaceful means are not possible, but still everyone prefers peaceful means.

C. Albert: *"I do not think that the United States believes that Taiwan is part of China. If the U.S. did, it would not have used the convoluted formula in the Shanghai Communique, saying that Chinese on both sides of the strait agree that Taiwan is part of China and that the United States does not challenge this position."*

Edward: The PRC insists that Taiwan is an internal Chinese problem, when in fact it is an international problem. What is the international status of Taiwan?

William: On the American side, this question received a great deal of attention during the Congressional debate on the Taiwan Relations Act. The end result is that the Act states that for purposes of domestic American law Taiwan is a country. But declaring Taiwan a country for domestic law purposes makes no statement about Taiwan's international status. This may be a lawyer's ploy to try to get around an impossible problem. But I think it does establish a conceptual base for treating Taiwan as something similar to a country in the international arena.

Albert: The State Department briefings after normalization did not use the term "international status" for Taiwan, but rather "international personality." The government position is that recognition or derecognition by the United States does not affect Taiwan's international personality. The specific example cited was that for 30 years we did not recognize the PRC, and yet it functioned as a government both domestically and internationally.

James: The State Department is attempting to treat Taiwan as a state in fact if not in law. This is not going to be totally successful. In the future I see increasing conflict between the Taiwan Relations Act and other international obligations of the United States. Domestic legislation cannot entirely avoid transnational effects.

Matthew: The PRC has protested the Taiwan Relations Act. Has it left open the possibility of protesting future United States involvement with Taiwan as interference with China's internal affairs?

William: The issue of Taiwan's status is still not entirely resolved. The United States is trying to be intentionally ambiguous about Taiwan's status, but over time we will be forced to be more and more explicit about whether Taiwan has international personality or is a province of China.

Because our relations with the PRC are pretty good at this point, I do not think we will have major clashes over important political matters. Instead, there will probably be a series of skirmishes over issues such as representation at scientific conferences, International Monetary Fund membership, and other similar things. Each of these will set a partial precedent.

Vincent: We have concentrated on the Taiwan problem from the point of view of the ROC, the PRC, and the Taiwan independence movement. But we also have to deal with the role of the United States, a factor that cannot be ignored.

I would urge the U.S. to take the following steps to promote the prospects for a peaceful solution. First, no weapons sales to the PRC. There have been too many examples in other areas of the world for us not to be concerned that arms sold to strengthen Chinese military capacities against the Soviet Union can be turned around and used against Taiwan. Second, and I will be very blunt, no support of any kind to the Taiwan independence movement. I say this with great sadness. Clearly there is good justification for the feelings of the Taiwan independence movement, but I do not see this group as an acceptable policy choice. The rejection of the independence movement will be conditioned on KMT acceptance of law and justice, elimination of martial law and torture—all of this to the extent possible. Let's face it, all governments have some problems along this line. If these conditions cannot be fulfilled, then I must withdraw my statement about not supporting the Taiwan independence movement.

Taiwan cannot count on anyone else, including the U.S. It must rely on itself. One aspect of promoting peace is to eliminate the possibility of a miscalculation by the PRC of its ability to take over Taiwan militarily. That means that Taiwan should build up its own military capability. It should buy weapons from the United States, West Germany, France, or whoever is willing to sell.

William: Arms sales and security present special problems. The Taiwan Relations Act makes strong statements about protecting Taiwan's security. The words spoken by the Administration, particularly last December, are also quite firm concerning the continued arms sales. The actions of the Administration, however, make me somewhat doubtful about this commitment.

For example, the original bill submitted by the Administration contained no security guarantee. The security provisions introduced by Senators Church and Javits were included in the bill in the face of considerable resistance by the Administration. Similarly, in testimony before the Congress, Administration spokesmen supported the principle of selling arms, but also seemed to resist the sale of specific weapons that appeared to be particularly useful.

Congress can allow or even urge the President to sell arms to Taiwan, but Congress cannot force the President to do so. We should watch what happens after the moratorium on arms sales ends in 1980. Even if the PRC strongly objects to renewed arms sales, we will probably do so anyway, but that is not a certainty.

I would like to say one word about the reference to human rights in the Act. As originally proposed by Senator Pell, the clause asked the American Institute in Taiwan to help foster the human rights of the majority of the people on Taiwan, meaning the Taiwanese. The Administration was quite upset. But it was able to change one key word, so that the Act now calls for fostering the human rights of *all* people on Taiwan. That change took the heart out of Senator Pell's proposal.

I do not think we should regard this clause as some kind of Congressional mandate; it is even less of a benchmark for what the Executive is likely to order officials in the American Institute to do.

Stephen: I just have this feeling that this clause might be used as a pretext by the Administration for not selling arms to Taiwan, on the ground that matters such as the Yu case violate human rights.

> D. *". . . both sides should take a more tolerant attitude on the question of single or dual representation in the international community."*

Frank: The Olympics may establish a pattern by which the two parties can deal with each other in international settings.[3] Let me read a *Time* reporter's interview with Chiang Ching-kuo, the full text of which was released by the Taiwan Government Information Office.[4]

> **Question:** With regard to the Olympics, the Republic of China has agreed to an arrangement of one-China, two-committees. Is that a sign that you are becoming more flexible?
>
> **Answer:** On the Olympic question, the guiding principle is that we are now a member country. We want to stay with the Olympic organization. The decision was made by the International Olympic Committee that they will have two committees, an Olympic Committee (Taipei) and an Olympic Committee (Peking). That was their decision, not one made by us. Our policy is simply to preserve our membership in

---

3   On the Olympics issue, see generally Dega Schembri & Ed McGonagle, *China and the 1980 Olympics,* The Asia Mail, Sept. 1979.
4   Free China Weekly, May 27, 1979. Excerpts were published in *Interview with Taiwan President,* Time, May 28, 1979, at 24.

the International Olympic Committee. It cannot be inter-
preted that we have made a compromise on the issue of one-
China.

The last is an important qualifier. I think the message is that if a
two-China approach is decided by *someone else*, Taiwan would
accept it.

We can draw some analogies from this. The United States may
adopt a two-China policy, but Taiwan will not take the initiative in
asking for such a stance. For example, if the United States had
wanted to normalize relations with the PRC, but had also wanted to
maintain official representation in Taipei, Taiwan would have accepted this arrangement since it would have been a decision made by
someone else.

My own feeling is that both sides should take a more tolerant
attitude on the question of single or dual representation in the
international community. Both sides have attended conferences and
academic meetings together. There will be additional opportunities to
do so in the future. Dual representation does not necessarily mean
that the possibility of future unification is wiped out.

Albert: In terms of external relations, we should encourage Taiwan to
establish some kind of liaison office with the PRC. This first step,
which will open up the channels of communication, can be taken
without dealing with other substantive issues.

Stephen: I think it is necessary to end the civil war status between the
PRC and Taiwan. To do that, the governing authority in Taiwan,
whether the Nationalists or some successor regime, ought to stop
challenging the legitimacy of the Peking regime on the Mainland. It
should concede that the Peking regime is the sole legal government of
China and that the authorities on Taiwan are merely the government
of Taiwan and the Pescadores. Taiwan should try to peacefully coexist
with the PRC, which will include having trade and cultural relations.

I am willing to entertain the idea of a so-called China commonwealth. The framework of a commonwealth of China could be
explored within the context of Vice-Premier Teng's statement that
Taiwan can maintain its own political and economic system so long as
it accepts the suzerainty of China. Taiwan could somehow recognize
the suzerainty of the big brother, and in this way establish a
connection with China at least in name, but still maintain an
independent political and military structure.

VI

PRC and ROC:
Dealing with Each Other

William: *We can all agree that we are dealing with a process of transition, although we may disagree about what the eventual outcome of the transition will or should be. Maybe the key notion is process. Not only will the solution take a long time, but the steps taken can be gradual and evolving rather than abrupt. Something that cannot be accomplished in one step may perhaps be attained in several steps over a period of time.*

Frank: Do you think it is too much to ask of Taiwan at this point to stop all provocative activities against the PRC, including propaganda, and even to stop claiming that it is the sole legitimate government of all of China?

Albert: I think it is. This question goes to the basic legitimacy of the government on Taiwan. The jobs of many people in the central government are tied to the concept of the ROC being the government of all of China, even if in reality they know this is not the case.

Matthew: Maybe something can be done. When I was in Taipei I saw some leaflets to be flown by balloon from Quemoy to the China mainland. The tone had changed quite a bit from the earlier "return to the Mainland" business. These materials contained a short story about a female worker in a factory. It talked about her life, her salary, her recreation, and nothing else. In other words, instead of using hard-sell slogans, Taiwan just presented a straightforward description of life in Taiwan that was quite effective. So it may not be too much to ask of Taiwan to stop using provocative words and phrases.

Charles: The PRC has already stopped the shelling of Quemoy and Matsu. Its press no longer refers to the "Chiang gang," but now says "Mr. Chiang." So China has already made some substantial moves toward reducing tension. But there has been no response from Taiwan; I think the next move now is up to Taiwan.

Albert: I think it takes two steps on China's part to get one step from Taiwan. Taiwan is such a small country. For example, if the *Central Daily News* stopped saying "Communist bandits," the KMT would lose the whole thing; that's all it has left.

From the American point of view it may seem paranoid to refuse to face reality, but if we are looking at the Chinese personality, we cannot use American standards. Look at the story of *Ah Q*.[1]

But I think you open up a very important area in suggesting a reduction of tension. We need to find a way where the first step toward reconciliation can be taken. It should include not just the PRC and the ROC, but also the Taiwan independence movement. I had not realized until this weekend the intensity and feeling of the people holding this position. Lawrence says he is prepared to give his life for the movement; that is a very strong statement. I believe fully in his sincerity. After many years in the United States, I have heard very few people say that they are willing to give their lives for any issue.

Stopping the shelling of the offshore islands is one step, but I think the PRC has to take an additional step, although I do not know what that should be. It is important for the PRC to provide the additional step. After all, it is the winner in this game. Only then can we say to the ROC, "Why don't you stop writing these propagandistic things? We know that they satisfy your own ego, but they don't mean anything anyway. They may help your psychological framework, but they don't make any sense."

George: I have listened very carefully to the entire discussion. I think we should realize that we have focused on what the ROC should do; it is always whether the ROC should do this or that. We are always making demands on the ROC.

But would it be too much to ask the PRC to drop Marxism? If we follow that line, there may be a chance of success.

---

1   Lu Hsun [Chou Shu-jen], *The True Story of Ah Q,* in Selected Stories of Lu Hsun 65-78 (3d ed. Peking 1972), criticizes some aspects of Chinese personality.

Charles: If Taiwan is willing to sincerely negotiate, China is willing to take 100 steps or even 1,000 steps. But, as you say, Taiwan is asking China to drop Marxism. That indicates a complete lack of sincerity.

A. *". . . if the other side calls you Mister, you should call them Mister in return."*

Vincent: I would urge Taiwan to adopt a flexible position, as well as to take the initiative. Taiwan has a flourishing economy, a relatively free society, a fairly confident population, and a standard of living that is way ahead of the Mainland. Consequently, it seems to me in Taiwan's interest to invite Mainland journalists and visitors to come to Taiwan. That puts the burden of reaction on the Mainland. In this way Taiwan would be saying, "We are perfectly happy for you to look at what we have accomplished under our political and social system. We think you might benefit from our system."

On a related matter, I realize that most of what we describe as the PRC's position is really Teng's position. I am not sure that, if he should die or fall from power, the next group of leaders would adopt the same flexible approach. Still, I think Teng has made a major concession in saying that if Taiwan will accept certain conditions concerning reunification, it may keep its political system for now. The very making of this statement is a larger concession than Premier Sun's condition that negotiations can begin only when the PRC drops Marxism.

The Mainland is not going to drop Marxism. It's like saying, "If only Taiwan would go Marxist, the PRC would be willing to talk with it."

Admittedly, Taiwan is much smaller and therefore has to hold a harder line. Still, the PRC has made most of the concessions so far. I think Taiwan should take the initiative to open up the channels of communication.

Stephen: I strongly agree. In the wake of normalization, Peking has made a number of gestures toward Taiwan by asking for trade, communication, and exchange of visits. In fact, some people in Taiwan, even within the leadership, have suggested responding to these actions. Unfortunately, there are other powerful people who are so stubborn or afraid of Communism that they are unwilling to do anything.

If PRC journalists came to Taiwan, perhaps their view of Taiwan would change. This kind of action would certainly help relax tensions.

Albert: It is very easy for us to favor this course of action, but Taiwan will not do it. Some people can exist only if their psychological beliefs are maintained. Once the beliefs fall through, the people are also through. Some of us may not understand this attitude because we are basing our analysis on American standards.

Time published excerpts from an interview with Chiang Ching-kuo.[2] The Chinese Information Agency released the complete text in which he was asked, "What do you have to lose? Get some PRC newsmen to see your prosperity and then you can convert them." Chiang in effect replied, "The only defense I have now is the psychological defense of this nation. I cannot talk to the PRC. If I do that, I will lose my psychological defense."

David: Taiwan has had so many frustrations on the international side that they are living in nonreality. It is as though someone who is really 150 pounds insists that he is 300 pounds; but we look at this person and know that he is only 150 pounds.

Chiang Ching-kuo says that without the psychological defense we might collapse. But this is not so. The KMT has always told the Taiwanese people that we will be finished when we are expelled from the United Nations, and again when the United States breaks diplomatic ties. But we still survive.

They now say that if we stop calling the other side "Communist bandits" we will be finished, but that is not so. I do not think you should call the other side bandits; that does not make you stronger or give you a psychological advantage. I think if the other side calls you Mister, you should call them Mister in return.

B. *". . . the ROC will be more concerned about internal than external problems."*

Henry: I do not think it is too much to ask the Taiwan government to drop its claim to all of the Mainland. For the next five years the ROC will be more concerned about internal than external problems. It fears internal changes, not actions by the PRC.

---

2   *Interview with Taiwan President,* Time, May 28, 1979, at 24.

What we need to find is some means of encouraging the Taiwan authorities to carry out reform. For example, can we get some kind of guarantee from the Taiwanese people, not from the ROC government, that the salaries of the present officeholders will be paid for their lifetimes if the KMT carries out a number of reforms, such as abandoning the return-to-the-Mainland policy? People on the island can then go about implementing meaningful political reform, while the present central government officials will not have to worry about their livelihoods.

Vincent: I do not agree that these fears simply reflect economic concerns. Guaranteed lifetime pensions would not solve anything. Power itself attracts people. Some kind of formula has to be found to give the present leadership a chance to stay in power, while at the same time enabling new people to attain a share of power.

William: Taiwan is in a dilemma. Its claim to being the government of all of China has been rejected internationally and scoffed at domestically. Yet any relaxation of its one-China position would raise internal problems concerning the legitimacy of the central government. The domestic consequences will make it difficult for Taiwan to back off its rhetorical position of one-China. Taiwan's domestic situation has been described as sitting on a volcano. It also has been clearly slipping internationally, particularly in the last seven years.

In such a difficult situation I think Taiwan has to take some risks. Instead, Chiang Ching-kuo talks about the maintenance of psychological defenses and holding on to past positions.

It seems to me that what Taiwan must do is to show some confidence in itself. If it thinks it has done well inside Taiwan, then it should be willing, even anxious, to show its accomplishments to the PRC. This is best achieved through direct contact. Taiwan talks about wanting peaceful competition with the PRC to see which is the better model. Well, Taiwan should go ahead and compete, rather than refuse to have any contacts.

Exhibiting confidence externally may produce some good internal consequences as well. At the time of normalization and during the last election, several of the opposition candidates criticized the government essentially for being incompetent in international affairs. But if the KMT can demonstrate competence, if it can reduce tensions (assuming that is the goal), if it can reestablish a place for itself under the sun—these actions will increase domestic support, rather than provoke greater challenges to its legitimacy.

C. *". . . the guiding principle should be reduction of tensions
between the two parties."*

Edward: I think the Peking leaders are facing a dilemma of tremendous proportions. They realize that the longer it takes to reintegrate Taiwan into China, the harder the process will be. But despite all the rhetoric and propaganda, they also realize that if current trends continue, the social, economic, and political gap between Taiwan and China will get wider and wider, and eventual reintegration will be that much more difficult.

On the other hand, if Peking tries to solve the Taiwan problem through drastic action, what drastic action can it take? Given Sino-Soviet tensions, the backward economy of China, and the fact that China lacks the amphibious capability to cross the Taiwan Strait, China cannot invade Taiwan. China might overrun Quemoy and Matsu and thus wipe out one-third of Taiwan's defense forces, but crossing the Taiwan Strait is another problem. American island-hopping experiences in World War II indicate that invading forces must have air and naval superiority and must also outnumber the defensive forces by at least two or three to one.[3] China may have naval superiority, but I am not so sure about its air power. It is not just a question of the number of ships and planes, but also their quality. The PRC can harass and really hurt Taiwan by a submarine blockade; but a successful blockade is not tantamount to military conquest.

So that is the dilemma. Peking wants to solve the Taiwan problem as quickly as possible because waiting will make the process

---

3   In the battle of Iwo Jima, the defending Japanese troops numbered 21,000. The U.S. Marine assault forces totaled 70,647; there were another 40,661 men in the Army garrison and Navy men assigned to duty ashore for a total expeditionary force of 111,308. If the crews of Admiral Turner's ships and Task Force 58 are added, the entire American force was over 250,000 men. Richard F. Newcomb, Iwo Jima 28-29 (1965). For the battle of Okinawa, the Japanese defending force was estimated to be about 50,000. On the American side, a total of 183,000 troops took part in the assault phase of the operation. This figure does not include all the forces in Admiral Nimitz's command which were marshalled in support of the operation. Roy E. Appelman, James M. Burns, Russell A. Gugeler & John Stevens, Okinawa: The Last Battle 15-26 (1948).

more difficult; however, it lacks the means with which to solve the problem quickly.

Frank: The policy of the United States toward Taiwan will play a major role in determining the continuation of separation or the pace of unification. To give an extreme example, if the United States says that it will keep its hands entirely off, I think the entire timetable would be greatly speeded up. Peking would step up military and economic pressure and there would be very little that Taiwan could do.

On the other hand, if the current legislation continues to be strongly supported by Congress and the Administration, I think there is very little Peking could do to push for unification. The status quo will remain for a long time. There will be some minor overtures, but very little substantial change.

If the process of solving the Taiwan problem is going to take a long time, what steps should Peking and Taipei take at this point? I believe that the guiding principle should be the reduction of tension between the two parties. We must suggest some concrete actions that both sides could take without losing face.

Philip: What we are discussing here is some reciprocal action between the Nationalists and the PRC. Peking's offer on trade and mutual visits has been regarded by many people as a step forward, but I do not see it that way. It is in fact a step backward. Conditions for "unification" offered by Vice-Premier Teng one-sidedly define the PRC as the national government and the ROC as a local government. That certainly scares many ROC leaders. Such conditions actually call for surrender of power by the KMT sooner or later.

Frank: I agree with what you say regarding the effect of Peking's actions. There will be difficulties so long as Peking insists that the ROC must change its flag, that is, give up its symbol of sovereignty. Moreover, tensions will not be reduced so long as the PRC continues to talk about reunification and refuses to renounce the use of force. Given these factors, I do not think that either the people or the government on Taiwan will respond.

At this point Peking should quietly drop the rhetoric of stressing peaceful unification or else, and also stop pressing for postal exchanges, visits, and trade. When the time is right, these kinds of contacts can readily emerge.

On Taipei's part, it has to make clear that it will engage in no hostile or provocative actions taken against China. All the hostile broadcasts, sending of balloons, and whatever sabotage or spy operations should be stopped immediately. It is within the capability of the Taiwan leadership to do these things.

James: A number of speakers have said that there is a consensus concerning the desire for a reduction of tensions around the Taiwan Strait. I think it is important for me to file a short dissent from that in order to make the picture more balanced.

As I see it, there is not very much tension in the strait at present. I agree that there is pressure on the KMT, both internationally and domestically, but not much of this is coming from the PRC. If we want the PRC to do something to reduce tension further at this point, there is not very much it can do.

When you ask officials in China how to resolve the Taiwan problem, they usually cite three major battles from the civil war. These are the Mukden, the Peking-Tientsin, and the Huai-hai campaigns.[4] In these three examples, there was only one instance of actual fighting between the two sides. Thus, the city of Peking was seized by Communist troops through a negotiated settlement between the Communist government and Fu Tso-yi. That is what PRC officials think of when they talk about a peaceful resolution of the Taiwan problem.

With that in mind, I really do not think that the PRC will be interested in reducing tensions. In fact, there may not be enough tension at present from its point of view. More pressure may have to be placed on the KMT officials to induce them to begin negotiations.

D. *"Do you want to liberate your brother by killing him?"*

William: Let me try to summarize some of our earlier discussions and also suggest some possible future developments. On the one hand, the PRC will try to make the prospect of unification attractive to Taiwan by encouraging visits, eliminating the use of harsh words, and so forth.

---

4   *See, e.g., Visiting Places of Revolutionary Significance: Chongqing, North Shaanxi, Xuzhou and Xibaipo,* Beijing Review, no. 39, pp. 7-19 (Sept. 28, 1979).

At the same time, the PRC will try at various points to increase pressure on the KMT in order to goad it toward the direction of unification. For example, if the ROC continues to maintain its one-China position, then the PRC may leave the status quo alone for a number of years. But several people have said the ROC might make some changes in its one-China stand in response to domestic pressure. In that case, the PRC must react to whatever steps the ROC takes. The more Taiwan moves toward separation, the greater will be the pressure exerted by the PRC. This might range from the use of harsher words, to increased economic pressure by trying to influence foreign businessmen, to pressure on the U.S. government to discontinue arms sales to Taiwan. There are many ways of directly bothering Taiwan short of an outright military assault. The issue can be fought out in a series of surrogate battles such as representation at the Olympics.

In sum, I see a dual scenario. On the one hand, I expect a continued use, or perhaps even an increase, of soft methods such as the proposed visits and trade. At the same time, I think the PRC seriously means that force might be used if the ROC heads down the road to separation. Ultimately, the goal is to make it so expensive for the ROC to be separate that it will consider reunifying with the PRC.

Stephen: Let me pose several ideas along a similar line, some of which are straw men intended to be knocked down.

Peking will not put too much pressure on Taipei for fear that Taipei will get desperate and do something drastic. Too much pressure might push Taiwan down the road to independence, toward the nuclear option, or toward the Russians. At the same time, there will be some kind of pressure exerted on Taipei. Vice-Premier Teng has said that if there is no possibility of the use of force, then the KMT will have no incentive to begin negotiations. So there will be some pressure, but not too much.

What can Peking do? One action is to continue efforts to isolate Taiwan diplomatically. This might include trying to get Saudi Arabia, South Korea, and other countries to break off diplomatic relations with Taiwan. There also can be some economic pressure. This might take the form of blacklisting American and other foreign companies dealing with Taiwan. The American Express boycott is a precedent. The success of this strategy will depend on Peking's own economic capability and attractiveness.

Let's say the PRC uses entirely peaceful methods for five or ten years without producing any great results—negotiations have not begun, and the trend toward separation appears to be more and more irreversible.

What will it do then? It may begin thinking about military action against Taiwan. We all know that even after ten years a frontal assault across the strait by Peking will not be feasible. In addition to military problems, Peking cannot afford to offend countries such as the United States and Japan. Of course, it is hard to predict the international situation ten years from now.

But there are other possible actions short of a direct military assault on Taiwan. Peking might try a blockade of Quemoy and Matsu. The goal would be to get the garrison to surrender, perhaps after a siege of six months or a year, when the garrison has run out of food and ammunition and also has been constantly bombarded by a psychological campaign to return to the motherland. Peking then can use these 60,000 or 70,000 prisoners of war as a basis for calling for serious negotiations between Peking and Taipei. Will the government and people on Taiwan have the stomach to continue resistance? If not, they must begin reunification on Peking's terms.

I think this latter scenario is quite feasible. Ten years from now the military balance between Taiwan and the PRC will have shifted even more in favor of the PRC. American military commitment to Taiwan may be much reduced. Although a blockade is a military action, not many lives need be lost. A siege does not require actual landings on the islands. It is an effort to stop the supply of arms and food.

There is another kind of possible blockade that requires even less force. China's submarine fleet could be used to stop foreign shipping to Taiwan on the ground that the PRC, as the government of China, has the legal authority to prevent foreign parties from dealing with a subordinate local unit, Taiwan. Such a blockade would lead to domestic political turmoil as well as to a possible economic collapse since Taiwan depends so much on foreign trade. In this kind of a situation, the PRC might call for negotiation or combine with certain elements in Taiwan.

Charles: The point is often made that China lacks the military capability to liberate Taiwan. Recently Vice-Premier Teng said the same thing. I think he made this statement to reassure Taiwan.

We are not military specialists, so we should not jump to conclusions about China's inability to attack Taiwan successfully. We should remember that in 1974 China said that the Formosan Strait is not an obstacle to the liberation of Taiwan. If something happens in Taiwan today, there are several things China can do. It has missiles; it can institute a blockade.

Albert: Or use nuclear weapons—you can destroy Taiwan by dropping one bomb. The question is not whether China has the capability, but whether it wants to use that power.

Matthew: We talk about liberation. Do you want to liberate your brother by killing him?

Vincent: I genuinely believe that at the present time there is no real military threat against Taiwan unless the whole world goes berserk. If you remember history, Hitler with all his power could not cross the English Channel. I also do not think that within the next few years the PRC will have the military capability of attacking Taiwan. Of course, it can send a suicide squad of 10,000 people who will get wiped out, but an attack will not be successful. To conquer Taiwan militarily is almost inconceivable.

E. *". . . suppose there is a drastic change of leadership on Taiwan and the new leaders are more opposed to unification."*

Philip: I do not think that Chinese policy toward Taiwan will change very much, except in the highly unlikely event of military provocation by the ROC. Peaceful appeals to Taiwan will continue, and may even intensify after the defense pact between the United States and the ROC expires in December.

An overseas Chinese who visited the PRC earlier this year said that Vice-Premier Li Hsien-nien told him the ROC government has three years to consider the offer made by Teng. I do not know whether this is true. In any case, I think that for the next few years the PRC will make direct appeals to the KMT leaders. The latter are not likely to respond unless something drastic happens on the domestic front.

There is a possibility of drastic political change in Taiwan. As the pressure for domestic reform grows, the PRC effort will shift toward trying to gauge the reactions of the Taiwanese politicians and the mainlander Chinese on Taiwan who are homesick. The PRC will try to promote a popular movement for unification. At the same time, the PRC will be cautious enough to avoid giving the KMT authorities a strong excuse for cracking down on the democratization movement. As the political opposition continues to press for major political reforms, some KMT leaders may come to realize that they must move in that direction as well. It is entirely possible that we will see a gradual move toward de facto independence, which eventually could solidify into a new de jure status. Because the process of transition would be gradual, it would not suddenly alarm Peking, leading it to take a drastic action to interfere.

The PRC presently thinks that the cause of unification will be best served if the KMT government does not feel threatened by elections and permits them to resume. Elections offer an open political forum for "unificationists" like Chen Ku-ying to speak out. At the same time, there may be Taiwan companies who would like to trade with the PRC. Many Mainlanders on Taiwan may also be eager to visit China. These are the kinds of things that conservative KMT leaders are worried about.

Frank: I find unconvincing the argument that pressure for unification will cause the KMT to make domestic changes more rapidly. This external threat will give the KMT all the more excuse to prolong its myths and control. Domestic change in Taiwan is a matter of grassroots political forces. If the KMT continues to refuse to change, I think there will be a sudden eruption. On the other hand, the KMT could take advantage of this local pressure for change to find means of assuring its own survival and continuity.

Stephen: I want to challenge one point. Some of us seem to assume, and the PRC seems to assume, that the democratization movement will ultimately work in favor of reunification. But suppose there is a drastic change of leadership on Taiwan and the new leaders are more opposed to unification. They may be Taiwanese who feel no particular attachment to the PRC. Consequently, Taiwan would move even further away from unification. If that does develop, the PRC is likely to turn to nonpeaceful means.

F. *"It is in China's interest that Chiang continues to occupy Quemoy and Matsu."*

Lawrence: I want to propose a specific step. If you want unification, the first thing to do is to solve the Quemoy and Matsu question. How?

Give these islands back to China. If you favor unification, you should support unifying Quemoy and Matsu with China. You should also support this move if you favor independence. Taiwanese do not think that Quemoy and Matsu are part of Taiwan's territory. Traditionally, they belong to China. If we do not solve this problem, China can attack these islands and capture 60-70,000 soldiers stationed there, brainwash them, and send them to attack Taiwan.

Vincent: I have quietly advocated for some time the abandonment of Quemoy and Matsu. But it is not a simple matter. It is an emotional issue, just as changing the flag is an emotional issue.

The arguments people in the KMT give for holding on to these two islands are totally unsupportable. They say that these islands will stop a Communist invasion of Taiwan. But Quemoy and Matsu can easily be bypassed; holding on to them will not stop an invasion. They say that these islands are part of Chinese territory, in particular, part of Fukien province. This fact is relevant only if you plan to go back to China. If you do not, then it is an anachronism.

I should add that these islands are only a small part of the larger problem. I would not favor simply giving them up without obtaining something in return, such as an indication that the PRC will take some new direction in its policy toward Taiwan.

I do not agree that if the Taiwan troops on those islands are captured, they will be brainwashed to come back to attack Taiwan.

George: To abandon or withdraw from Quemoy and Matsu is impossible at this time. Such an action will complicate the issue by introducing many new problems. I doubt that withdrawal would adequately serve as a gesture of good will or a show that Taiwan is willing to mind its own business. Peking would not be satisfied by just this one step.

Lawrence: I would like to ask those familiar with the PRC's position: Is the PRC interested in recovering Quemoy and Matsu?

Charles: The PRC does not see the Quemoy and Matsu problem as isolated from the overall Taiwan problem.

In the late 1950s Chiang was pressured by the Eisenhower Administration to withdraw from these islands in return for an American guarantee of the security of Taiwan. The United States already had a two-China policy of trying to isolate Taiwan from mainland China. Chiang resisted from the very beginning. But the pressure was very great, and finally he had to agree to withdraw. When China heard about this, it helped Chiang to stay by beginning the bombing of Quemoy and Matsu. Chiang then could say to the United States, "Now that China is bombing the islands, we cannot withdraw in the face of pressure."

It is in China's interests that Chiang continues to occupy Quemoy and Matsu. This occupation symbolizes that Taiwan is still part of China. This is what I mean when I say that Quemoy and Matsu are not isolated from the entire China problem.

Albert: It is true that in the late 1950s Chiang was ready to give up the islands in exchange for the security of Taiwan, but China did not want this to happen. China would want the islands if the transfer were not linked to guarantees concerning the security of Taiwan. But a transfer tied to the security of Taiwan would be rejected by China.

Quemoy and Matsu are not the issue. The Chinese are not interested in those two small islands. They are interested in Taiwan.

Lawrence: Are you saying that the PRC will not even allow the KMT to give up Quemoy and Matsu unless Taiwan and the Pescadores also come along with them?

Charles: If the KMT withdraws from the islands, of course China will take them.

Lawrence: But the KMT can take steps to remove troops from Quemoy and Matsu anytime it wishes. Will the PRC use military force to stop the withdrawal?

Robert: If a government is really committed to territorial integrity, then the recovery of even an inch of land is important. I do not think any government would refuse land that was just offered to it. I cannot imagine why Peking would use military force to stop a withdrawal.

Lawrence: I strongly suspect that Peking wants to hold these two islands as hostages. A withdrawal might be regarded as a step toward a two-China policy or an independent Taiwan.

James: My guess is that Peking will probably take over the islands if the KMT leaves. But the important issue is whether the KMT will leave. Withdrawal would put the legitimacy of the KMT government into question.

VII

Reducing Tensions

Matthew: *All of the scenarios we have discussed so far involve conflict and confrontation, and end with bloodshed. We are here at this conference as overseas Chinese scholars not beholden to any government. We have the moral obligation to say what we would like to see by way of process and result. Therefore, I am going to speak, perhaps in a tone of wishful thinking, about what I hope will happen.*

Matthew: I would like to see China and all Chinese living under peaceful conditions, probably as a unified country; but we should never rule out a minority's opinion, especially a minority concentrated in one area. We should never abuse majority rule to foreclose the right of a group of people to make its own decisions on one matter or another.

Whether under conditions of unification or separation, a basic consideration is that there should be no conflict, no more bloodshed between brothers, whether across the strait or within Taiwan. I also would like to see our people's lives improved both economically and politically, no matter which side they live on.

Time is a very important factor here. I do not think the PRC is in a great hurry to reunify the country. I also think that patience will lead us to a better result. A hasty effort will make the reunion an unhappy one. If China tries to force the other side into submission, it may end up with a situation in which it has gulped down 17 million unwilling people who will resent it forever. That would be no good for China, or for the human race.

We have seen in the past that China has been divided many, many times, sometimes for several hundred years. But that does not matter in the long run. We also learn from history that a forced unification, such as in the case of Ireland, may lead to long years of unceasing hostility, bloodshed, and anarchy.

Moreover, for now the PRC cannot take any practical military action against Taiwan. At the same time, Taiwan is sitting next to a great big country like China, and has no realistic alternative but to establish some sort of ties with it. But that will not happen until the standard of living in the PRC has been upgraded to a level close to Taiwan's. Until that day comes I do not think that reunification can be anything other than paper talk.

Consequently, in this period before the final settlement, we should look for some kind of coexistence under the condition of separation. I think as overseas Chinese we should remind our two governments across the strait that they have a great many jobs to do. To reunite Taiwan and China is an important job indeed, but it is not an issue of immediate moment.

One of the important jobs for the Taiwan government is to make itself more representative of the Taiwan people so that it can act as a spokesman for this group in the future. Economic accomplishments have been good, but that is not all there is to it. There are a lot of other areas to be addressed: social justice, human rights, and especially broader political participation.

The PRC government also has many things to do. The standard of living in China is perhaps one of the worst in the world. The ideals of political participation and human rights are by no means honored. There is also the big job of carrying out the four modernizations. Confronted by all these great tasks, the PRC ought not to spend energy and resources to build up tension just for the sake of uniting Taiwan and the Mainland.

To exercise restraint takes willingness and wisdom. The willingness can be developed only if the PRC has a historical consciousness that looks many generations into the future. Years from now people will look back and say that in the twentieth century people did poorly or did well.

In this spirit, I would like to suggest a course of action for the two sides. I propose a moratorium for 10, 20, or 30 years during which neither side will make any gesture or threat about reunification. Let the situation calm down. Let Chinese people on both sides of the strait compete to see who can do better, until both sides reach comparable levels of living standard and political freedom.

But we cannot just sit and hope that the two governments will agree to wait. We Chinese living outside of China and Taiwan have a special privilege. We can speak to both sides with equal eloquence and persuasion and without stigma. It is our responsibility to tell both sides during the moratorium to reduce hostilities and not to make any empty gestures. Let us not fight; let us cool down.

By listening to overseas scholars speak, Peking can back off without loss of face. Perhaps we should ask a third party such as Lee Kuan-yew to endorse the idea. He is ethnically but not politically Chinese, and heads the largest Chinese community outside of Chinese territory. Other third parties can help to establish communication during the cooling period. We could try to set up an institute in Hong Kong to train Mainland technicians and engineers with Taiwan technology. This kind of thing can be done. It saves face on both sides, and the Chinese are people who love face.

In reality, we cannot expect Peking or Taipei to agree explicitly to this moratorium. We might try to get 50 or 100 signatures and take an ad in the *New York Times* announcing the moratorium and asking both sides not to contradict it. Some other people would then, through prearrangement, come to support the statement.

Question: Are there historical precedents for this kind of moratorium?

Matthew: Not in Chinese history. But there were de facto moratoriums in the dealings between the Chin [1115-1234A.D.] and the Sung [960-1279 A.D.]. And in the Nan-Pei Ch'ao [Northern and Southern dynasties, 317-589A.D.] a verbal war was carried on for quite a while and then cooled off, eventually leading to an exchange of ambassadors.

William: There are things going on in the international arena that make a moratorium almost impossible, including such seemingly simple issues as who shows up at the Olympics or who gets landing rights at which airport. The resolution of these small issues will constantly pose the bigger issue of the status of Taiwan.

More importantly, the KMT government may be willing to keep quiet; but there is a political dynamic inside Taiwan that will continue to churn. I do not know what direction this dynamic will take—

independence or drastic change or gradual reform—but something probably will happen that will upset a moratorium.

In substance, the moratorium favors only the KMT because it calls for freezing the status quo. In fact, it is a cleverly disguised way of arguing for no change at all. For example, the opposition in Taiwan would likely be against this approach because it would inhibit any effort to bring about change. After all, whenever a proposal is made for reform, the KMT could resist by saying that the change would violate the moratorium and provoke the PRC. The PRC also has no particular interest in adhering to a moratorium. It has nothing to lose by keeping a moderate level of pressure constantly on Taiwan.

Moreover, the moratorium idea presupposes that the two sides are more or less equal. But we do not have a situation of two equals here. I think the KMT must realize that it is in a great deal of trouble and cannot propose ideas that presuppose equal bargaining positions.

Lawrence: As a Taiwanese I oppose the moratorium. The reasons are very simple. If we were to accept this proposal, we would continue to live under the fear of being taken over by China. In addition, we would continue to be oppressed by the KMT regime.

Matthew: The moratorium does not mean that we endorse the present regime forever. After the moratorium is over, self-determination can still be carried out. The point of the moratorium is to reduce hostilities in the meantime.

Perhaps "moratorium" is the wrong word. What I have in mind is a pledge of no violence plus a pledge for reduction of tension. I do not mean to exclude domestic political change on either side during the moratorium. I do not think the end result will be that only one party gains some time or some advantage.

One effect of the moratorium could be to set a time limit within which the reformers could ask for something to be done on Taiwan. The clock is ticking, and the KMT must do something before time runs out. The reformers can move ahead with a timetable and in a well-planned way. For example, if major changes occur within one year, the opposition will not have enough time to develop a shadow cabinet. If it gets five or ten years time, it can develop a shadow government from the president down to a county commissioner.

For the PRC, the moratorium could reduce the possibility of conflict along the southern coast. This is important because there is a danger of conflict along the northern border with the Soviet Union at any time. Any kind of reduction of tension along the coast would help. Moreover, the time and money saved could be invested in the modernization drive. It is even possible that some human resources from Taiwan might be funneled to the PRC through third channels. If there were tension and conflict, the PRC could not call on Taiwan's assistance in this regard.

This kind of thing will not happen right away. But, in the longer term, the reduction of tension could lead to such a result. In the short term, the removing of rhetorical saber-rattling could substantially increase the chances for negotiations, and eventual rapprochement.

Vincent: I am very attracted to the suggestion of a moratorium. I have never heard it before. In a way, it is like a laissez-faire system where each side proves itself by actions rather than words.

My problem is that I find a number of operative objections to this proposal. What you are really arguing for is that the KMT would run Taiwan for the indefinite future. The freezing of the status quo, which essentially is what a moratorium is, would require that the PRC say nothing about its wish to reunify Taiwan eventually under its own aegis. It also means that for the time being the Taiwan independence movement should cease operating. This is contrary to the interests of both groups. If there is some way to convince the PRC and the Taiwan independence movement that a moratorium would not be against their interests, maybe there is a chance of it working.

Another factor we should consider involves ideology. A moratorium would ask diehards in Peking to give up the job of completing the revolution, and diehards in Taiwan to give up the task of challenging Maoism and rescuing their compatriots on the Mainland.

Matthew: It is exactly because scholars do not have any kind of power base, but only a moral position, that the moratorium idea has a chance. Both Peking and Taipei may feel caught in their own rhetorical traps. By asserting a moral position, scholars may provide the rationale for backing off from these traps.

George: I also believe that a moratorium is a practical measure to take at this stage. Let us cool things down. It would provide the people, not the elite groups but the people, a chance to sort through their ideas. Today, I think a lot of us need more time to rethink our own positions.

Let me tell you my fundamental approach. I do not believe that the leaders in Peking ought to have the right to dictate the terms on the Taiwan question.

A. *"[Is nationalism] the only basis, or the most legitimate basis,
for resolving the Taiwan problem?"*

Frank: I agree with the approach that we must distinguish between
the rhetoric and the underlying reality. Both sides talk about unification, although each has its own version of what that term entails. At
this point, I consider both sets of rhetoric irrelevant.

What is the reality then? The reality is that China is divided into
two parts, both of which have been operating as separate, independent entities for the past 30 years. The problem confronting us is
that there exists great tension between the two sides. It is not
productive for us to argue in general terms about whether Taiwan
should or should not be reunited with the Mainland. Our object
should be to find what kinds of methods can reduce tensions between
the two sides.

The current Taiwan problem is more complicated than the
continuation of the pre-1949 civil war. In terms of action, the civil war
ended 30 years ago. Peace and stability have persisted there; that is a
fact.

When you get to the guts of the issue, the reunification argument
is based on nationalism—on the belief that all of China should be
united as one country and one nation.

We are here not as politicians but as intellectuals. As such, we
should be concerned not with questions of pursuing political power,
but rather with tougher moral issues involving basic values. If we are
to make a contribution, it is by raising the question of whether
nationalism is the only basis, or the most legitimate basis, for
resolving the Taiwan problem. Is nationalism sufficient justification
for the PRC to take drastic and costly actions against Taiwan?

If the fundamental issue is whether China should be a single
national unit, then considerations about the well-being of the people
are assigned a secondary position. But if Peking adopts a set of
priorities that makes the well-being of the people the primary
concern, then I think the whole development of its Taiwan policy
would be different.

Let me be more specific. There are four factors affecting
attitudes toward the Taiwan problem: the nationalistic sentiment for
unification; a desire to implement some ideological goals; the pursuit
of power; and what I would characterize as concern for the well-being
of the people.

If you are motivated by nationalism and put unification as your highest priority, then you will unify at any cost. If you are obsessed with ideological goals, then Taiwan and the PRC should fight to the death in order to establish Communism or the Three-People's-Principles. But, to me, clearly the most important values are peace and the well-being of the people. These are the top priorities, not the other factors.

I say again: The task of the intellectual is to argue on moral and intellectual bases and persuade leaders in Peking and Taipei why it is important to make well-being and peace the highest priorities. If we do not do this, but instead frame our thinking according to the premises set by the politicians, then I think we will have failed.

Charles: How can you separate peace from reunification? There will be no peace in the area without unification.

Frank: If the political leaders can be convinced that the well-being of the people should have the highest priority, then it does become possible to have peace without unification. That is obviously asking these leaders to make major changes in their thinking. But that is precisely our task.

For example, China is now talking about the four modernizations as the highest priority for the nation. That means to improve the people's standard of living, to achieve more equitable distribution of wealth, and to develop industry, agriculture, and science and technology. (I would not include modernization of the military.) If these things can be done, China could make a tremendous contribution, not only to the one billion Chinese, but also to the whole world.

I would strongly argue that the Chinese leadership should be urged to see the great value of simply taking good care of one quarter of the human race. If you compare this value to the value of unifying with Taiwan, it is absolutely clear in my mind that all the resources should be devoted to the first task. Unification may be a desirable goal, but in terms of priority, it should not be the first one.

If in the course of securing well-being and peace, you can also achieve unification, that is fine. But I believe it is intellectually unsound to turn it around and say that China must unify with Taiwan at any cost.

Charles: There is enormous linkage among the four factors you mentioned. For example, perhaps China's involvement in the Vietnam war of the 1960s withdrew resources from the modernization effort. But to not take part in the war would in turn have adversely affected the effort to modernize, particularly in the long term. The same thing applies to power. If the present leadership does not have the power, how can it carry out modernization?

Frank: But linkage is not the same thing as priority. We all know that these things are linked. But the question is the setting of priorities.

David: I do not know much about ideology or power. But I am highly concerned with well-being and peace. People may talk about national purpose, but what they are really concerned with is their work, where their sons are going—the practical aspects of life.

Politicians try to use the concepts of well-being and peace. They say that unification will serve well-being and peace. When looking at the issue of well-being, we should look past the political rhetoric and instead examine how any change would actually affect the lives of the people.

B. ". . . *the importance of maintaining a cultural alternative.*"

Matthew: I have heard a different kind of argument that goes beyond the notion of well-being as measured by standard socioeconomic criteria. Many Chinese intellectuals, both overseas and in Taiwan, talk about the importance of maintaining a cultural alternative.

We tend to be preoccupied with the political aspects of being a nation. I would prefer to see a nation defined in cultural terms. In talking about culture, I do not mean merely preserving museum items, though unfortunately that is the definition often used by governmental authorities. By culture I mean organizing a way of life.

In the PRC it seems that the individual is subjugated to the will of the larger society. Taiwan is trying some other means that perhaps will be valuable for the world in the future. Taiwan is attempting to cope with American individualism on the one hand and with the socialistic framework of the Three-People's-Principles on the other. Will it find some way of synthesizing collectivism with individualism, drawing on the best of both? Is there a third alternative for the world that is neither total individualsim nor total statism?

For example, the government carried out land reform, but did not follow up with organizing the farmers into collectives or communes. Nevertheless, farmers voluntarily organized some collectives based on the kind of mutual help developed in China over the centuries: mutual assistance and sharing of resources among kinship groups and neighbors.

This kind of alternative should be allowed to develop. It can be useful not only for China but also for many other nations. It should inspire other nations to think that there are not only two kinds of values, American ones and Russian ones. I find very persuasive the point that Taiwan should be preserved separately from China because it has a very distinct way of life and provides a different cultural alternative.

Vincent: Matthew's definition of culture resembles that of an anthropologist. I would like to talk about a narrower definition of culture, concerning creative arts, literature, and the realm of thought.

I have always been saddened by the fact that those controlling intellectual life in Taiwan have always taken a very negative and strait-jacketed approach to culture. For example, just because the Mainland favors the simplification of characters, Taiwan is against it. But surely the simplification of characters is a problem people have grappled with for two generations before the Communists did anything about it.

Another example is Confucianism. Because the Mainland authorities have attacked Confucianism, the KMT upholds it as though it has no faults. I remember that my parents' generation and my generation fought against Confucianism because it contained certain defects.

What I am trying to say is that I think Taiwan can serve as an alternative cultural model both in the larger sense of a way of life and in the narrower sense of creative expression. But Taiwan should make decisions on their merits rather than just say, "What do Communists do? Whatever they do, we are against it." That is a reactionary stance.

Edward: My optimal scenario may also be wishful thinking. Neither government has the capability to implement its rhetorical policy goals. Yet both continue to distort their priorities by investing huge resources to build up a military capability in support of their unrealistic policy goals. The people on both sides of the strait consequently suffer, without even being able to question the wisdom of these goals.

In order to break the deadlock, I think there should be a mutual reduction of forces to reduce tensions in the Formosan Strait. Specifically, I would like to see the ROC withdraw troops from

Quemoy and Matsu; in return the PRC would reduce its already very thin forces opposite those islands. The ROC should also declare that it has no hostile intentions with respect to China and will not try to recover China by military means, and the PRC should declare that it will not attempt to reunify China by military means.

Limited exchange and communications in the form of trade and visits should begin. This is the first step toward reduction of misunderstanding and mistrust. We should call upon the two sides to peacefully coexist and work toward social, economic, and political modernization. Let me emphasize the political modernization aspect: respect for human rights, an increase in genuine political partici- pation, much greater accountability of the government elite to the people, and implementation of the rule of law and not just the traditional rule by law. There are too many government elites intent on implementing their own versions of utopia, whether Marxism or the Three-People's-Principles, without taking into consideration the well-being of the people. In history, the greatest harm often has been caused by political elites with good intentions. The more utopian their vision and intense their commitment, the greater the harm.

Finally, since the conflict cannot be resolved by the present generation, let the future generations decide for themselves. After 15 or 30 or 100 years the gap between the ROC and the PRC may be reduced. The current elites on both sides are very passionate; they have their own psychological hangups on this issue. If they cannot solve this problem or can only solve it at tremendous cost, then I think the answer is to cool the whole thing off for the time being. The same options that we have discussed concerning autonomy or indepen- dence or reunification will still be there in the future. Let us not try to decide now what we are unable to decide and to resolve. Let the future generations decide and resolve these questions for them- selves. In short, there really is no short term solution; hence I am also for the moratorium.

Philip: Many of the issues raised here involve the question of timing. I think there is a growing number of people within the KMT, both Mainlander and Taiwanese, who would argue for speeding up the process. I really feel that the problem of constitutional reform must be resolved very soon.

Afterword

Edward: What can we do? A conference like this enables people having different points of view and sentiments to come together for open and sincere exchanges. Through frank discussions, we may be able to come up with some new understanding, perhaps not a consensus, but some new approaches toward how to solve this problem. The best contribution we can make is to speak our consciences without hesitation.

We have no guns, we have no troops; we will have to work in the realm of ideas. I welcome the opportunity. At least two of the parties do have guns and troops, and yet they are not able to make any progress.

Appendix

Appendix 1

Trong R. Chai is Associate Professor of Political Science at Medgar Evers College, City University of New York, where his research centers on public administration and political science. He is a native of Taiwan. In 1970, he helped found World United Formosans for Independence, and served as the first president of that organization.

Winberg Chai is Vice President for Academic Affairs at the University of South Dakota. He previously was chairman of the Humanities Division and of the Department of Asian Studies at City College, City University of New York.

Professor Chai was born in Shanghai in 1934, and later went to Taiwan where he completed high school. He came to the United States in 1955. He is a frequent visitor to the ROC and also visited the PRC in 1973.

Professor Chai writes widely in the fields of political science and Asian studies. His publications include: *The Search for a New China: A Study of History, Leadership and Politics of the Chinese Communist Party* (1975); *The Foreign Relations of the People's Republic of China* (1972); *Essential Works of Chinese Communism* (1969).

Parris Hsu-cheng Chang is Professor of Political Science at Pennsylvania State University. His research interests include comparative politics, international relations, and American foreign policy.

Professor Chang was born in 1936 in Chiayi, Taiwan. After receiving his B.A. from the Taiwan National University, he came to the United States in 1961, and received his Ph.D. in 1969 from

Columbia University. He taught at the University of Michigan before assuming his present position in 1972. He has traveled to the PRC on several occasions.

Professor Chang's publications include: *Power and Policy in China* (2d ed. 1978); *Radicals and Radical Ideology in China's Cultural Revolution* (1973); "What Taiwan Can Do," *Newsweek*, January 22, 1979.

Pi-chao Chen is Professor of Political Science at Wayne State University. His principal areas of scholarly interest are demography, Chinese population studies, and Chinese politics. He has visited the PRC on a number of occasions in connection with his research on population.

Professor Chen was born in Taichung, Taiwan, graduated from Tunghai University in 1959, and came to the United States in 1961. He received his Ph.D. in political science from Princeton University in 1966.

Professor Chen serves as consultant to many health and population organizations. His publications include: *The Health and Population in the People's Republic of China* (1976); "The Planned Birth Program of the People's Republic of China, with a Brief Analysis of Its Transferability," *SEADAG Papers on Problems of Development in Southeast Asia* (November 1975).

Tan S. Chen is the president of the Taiwanese Association of America. He was born in Tainan, Taiwan, and received a B.S. from Taiwan National University and a Ph.D. in geosciences from Purdue University. He is employed by the United States Department of Commerce.

Samuel C. Chu is Professor of History and director of the East Asian Program at Ohio State University. He was born in 1929 in Shanghai and came to the United States in 1941. He studied at Dartmouth College and at Columbia University, where he received his Ph.D. in history in 1958. Prior to joining Ohio State in 1969, he taught at the State University of New York at New Paltz, Bucknell University, and the University of Pittsburgh.

Professor Chu's scholarly interests focus on late Ch'ing and early Republican China. He is the author of *Reformer in Modern China:*

Chang Chien, 1853-1926 (1965), *Passage to the Golden Gate* (1967), and many articles and reviews. Professor Chu also is active in scholarly and cultural organizations concerned with Chinese matters. He visited the ROC on a number of occasions, and the PRC in 1975.

Kuang-huan Fan is Professor of Political Science at the State University of New York at Cortland and chairman of that department in 1972-1976. He was born in Taiwan in 1932. He received his A.B. from Bethel College in 1956 and his Ph.D. in political science from New York University in 1963. Prior to assuming his present post, he taught at the University of Idaho and the College of Great Falls.

Professor Fan's research interests focus on Chinese politics. His publications include: *From the Other Side of the River* (1975); *Mao Tse-tung and Lin Piao: Post-Revolutionary Writings* (1972); *The Chinese Cultural Revolution: Selected Documents* (1968). He has visited the PRC a number of times.

Cho-yun Hsu has been Professor of History and Sociology at the University of Pittsburgh since 1970. He was born in Amoy, Fukien, in 1930, and went to Taiwan at the age of 18. He received a B.A. in 1953 and an M.A. in 1956 from the Taiwan National University and a Ph.D. in history from the University of Chicago in 1962. He returned to teach at the Taiwan National University in 1962, and was chairman of the Department of History from 1965 to 1970.

Professor Hsu is an internationally known authority on ancient China. His publications include: *The Han Agriculture* (forthcoming); *Anthology of Studies in Ancient China* (1967); *Ancient China in Transition* (1965); *Introduction to Historical Research* (1965).

Che-tsao Huang is Director and Associate Professor, Center for Educational Technology at York College, City University of New York. He specializes in the field of communications, particularly film, television and educational technology. He was the president of the Council of Educational Communications and Technology of the City University of New York in 1973-74.

Professor Huang was born in Taoyuan, Taiwan in 1938, graduated from Chung Hsiung University in Taiwan, and arrived in the U.S. in 1964. He received his M.A. and Ph.D. degrees from Indiana University. While not a China specialist by training, he has traveled widely in the PRC.

Thomas W. Huang is a lawyer in private practice in Boston, specializing in immigration, corporate, and international business law. Dr. Huang was born in Taiwan, and graduated from Taiwan National University with a B.A. in law in 1964. He served as a Judge-Advocate in the ROC army, and was a foreign service officer in the Ministry of Foreign Affairs from 1965 to 1967. After coming to the United States, Dr. Huang graduated from Indiana University Law School in 1970, and received his LL.M. in 1971 and S.J.D. in 1975 from Harvard Law School. He is a member of the Massachusetts and District of Columbia bars.

Dr. Huang is active in Chinese community affairs and has a special interest in Sino-American relations. He also has written several articles on Chinese law.

Tzu-Min Kao is a specialist in physical medicine and rehabilitation. He is a graduate of Kaohsiung Medical College in Taiwan and has done post-graduate work at New York University Medical Center and at the University of Washington in Seattle. Dr. Kao presently is Director, Physical Medicine, Jefferson Memorial Hospital; Associate Professor of Health Sciences, George Washington University School of Medicine; and Clinical Assistant Professor of Physical Medicine, Georgetown University School of Medicine. He is also Executive Director of the Taiwan Benevolent Association of America, a non-political organization of American citizens which helps new immigrants from Taiwan to adjust to American society.

Michael Ying-mao Kau is Professor of Political Science at Brown University. He was born in Taiwan in 1934. He received a B.A. from Taiwan National University in 1956, and an M.A. in 1960 and a Ph.D. in politics in 1966 from Cornell University. He has been teaching at Brown University since that time.

Professor Kau's research activities have concentrated in the fields of comparative government, Chinese politics, and political development. His publications include: *The Lin Piao Affair: Power Politics and Military Coup* (1975); *The People's Liberation Army and China's Nation-Building* (1973); *The Political Work System of the Chinese Communist Military* (1971). He also is the director of Mao's Writings Project at Brown, and editor of *Chinese Law and Government.*

Professor Kau is a member of the National Policy Panel to Study

U.S.-China Relations, United Nations Association. He has visited the PRC on several occasions.

Victor Hao Li is Lewis Talbot and Nadine Hearn Shelton Professor of International Legal Studies at Stanford University. From 1974-76 he was Director of the Center for East Asian Studies at Stanford. Professor Li was born in China in 1941 and came to the United States six years later. He received a B.A. and J.D. from Columbia and an S.J.D. from Harvard Law School. He is a member of the New York Bar. Prior to joining the Stanford faculty, he taught at Michigan Law School and Columbia Law School.

Professor Li's research interests center on political-legal work in the People's Republic of China and public international law. He is a consultant to the U.S. Senate Committee on Foreign Relations. He has visited the PRC a number of times.

His publications include *Law and Politics in China's Foreign Trade* (1977); *Law Without Lawyers: A Comparative View of Law in China and the United States* (1977); *De-Recognizing Taiwan: The Legal Problems* (1977).

Hung-mao Tien is Professor of Political Science at the University of Wisconsin and also is associated with the university's Land Tenure Center. He was born in a small agricultural village in Taiwan in 1938, and graduated from Tunghai University in 1961. He came to the United States in 1963 on an academic exchange program, and received his M.A. in 1966 and Ph.D. in 1969 from the University of Wisconsin. He has taught at that institution since 1968; from 1975 to 1978 he was chairman of the Center System Department of History and Political Science.

Professor Tien is the author of *Government and Politics in Kuomintang China, 1927-37* (1972) and is a frequent contributor to political science and Asian studies journals. He is also an editor of *Taiwan shih-pao* [Taiwan Times], a newspaper published in Kaohsiung, Taiwan. He visited the PRC in 1973.

Richard Yang is Professor of Chinese Studies at Washington University in St. Louis. He was born in Shansi, China in 1924, and grew up during World War II and the civil war. He graduated from National Central University in 1947.

Professor Yang's research deals with Chinese language and literature; he is the author of numerous books and articles on these subjects. In addition, he is a specialist in American foreign policy. Professor Yang is a frequent traveler to the Republic of China, most recently in 1979 as Visiting Professor at Taiwan National University. His publications include *Arthur H. Vandenberg and the Senate Foreign Relations Committee* (1966); *The Chinese World* (1978); *The World of Asia* (1979).

Appendix 2

A. **Statement of Hungdah Chiu,** Professor of Law, University of Maryland School of Law. (Based on a speech delivered at the University of Virginia School of Law, Oct. 1979.)

In the statement accompanying the Joint Communique on Establishment of Diplomatic Relations between the United States and the PRC, President Carter stated that "the United States continues to have an interest in the peaceful resolution of the Taiwan issue and *expects* that the Taiwan issue will be settled peacefully by the Chinese themselves." (Emphasis added.) The parallel PRC statement reaffirmed its position that reunifying Taiwan with the Mainland is "entirely China's internal affair." The Carter Administration took the public position that the PRC statement did not contradict the U.S. stand on a peaceful settlement of the Taiwan issue. This position, unfortunately, is unrealistic. It is elementary, from a legal and a political viewpoint, that a country may use force in conducting its internal affairs, for example, to quell a local insurrection. Thus, the Carter statement on a peaceful resolution of the Taiwan issue was, in fact, implicitly rejected by the PRC. Subsequently, Vice-Premier Teng Hsiao-ping's statements of January 5 and 30, 1979 further confirmed the PRC's insistence on the right to resort to force to invade Taiwan. (*See Peking Says Taiwan Can Keep Autonomy Under Unification,* New York Times, Jan. 10, 1979, at A8, col. 5; *Teng, on Capitol Hill, Says Peking Must Keep Taiwan Options Open, id.,* Jan. 31, 1979, at A1, col. 3.)

With respect to the security of Taiwan, the Carter Administration's public position has been that any PRC military attack against

Taiwan is extremely unlikely for the foreseeable future, primarily because the PRC has limited amphibious capacity. In addition, such an attack would reverse the PRC's political gains in the West, thus jeopardizing continued U.S. help for the PRC's modernization program.

This view is unfortunately short-sighted. The assertion that the PRC lacks the amphibious capacity for a successful invasion of Taiwan may be *partially* true today, but the PRC is currently in the midst of an intensive modernization drive to upgrade its military capability, including, of course, amphibious capability. Moreover, an invasion of Taiwan could be undertaken without a large-scale amphibious landing on the island. The PRC's 5000-plane air force has an obvious numerical superiority over the 300-plane air force of the ROC. If the PRC decided to invade Taiwan, it could destroy the ROC air force, including its limited land-to-air missile air defense system, within a few days or at most a few weeks, thus ensuring air superiority over the Taiwan Strait. Once the Taiwan Strait was secured, the PRC could use a few marine and airborne divisions to occupy a port in Taiwan. It then could establish a safe air and maritime corridor between the occupied Taiwan port and a Mainland port for the transport of an invading force. (The PRC navy, with its 50 submarines, is generally believed to be superior to that of the ROC.) Thus, the security of Taiwan is essentially dependent on its maintaining air superiority over the Taiwan Strait.

Ideally, Taiwan should have a limited strategic deterrent force to attack Mainland air bases in Fukien, Kiangsi, Kuangtung and Chekiang provinces and some industrial complexes such as Shanghai. However, the Carter Administration has apparently eliminated the possibility of providing even very limited strategic weapons to Taiwan. In this situation, the best Taiwan can hope for is to maintain air superiority over the Taiwan Strait through use of high-performance military aircraft which can overcome the numerical superiority of the PRC air force. However, the Carter Administration has so far been reluctant to sell high-performance military aircraft to the ROC. If future administrations also follow this policy, Taiwan's defense capability will gradually deteriorate.

Technologically and economically, Taiwan could in theory develop its own weapons industry, but the country is unlikely to reach the stage of integrated manufacturing, as opposed to assembling of sophisticated military aircraft. Even if Taiwan were technologically

able to manufacture such aircraft, the high cost of weapons development would severely strain the island's economic growth, with
ensuing social and political problems.

Taiwan cannot turn to the Soviet Union to get high-performance
military aircraft, since it is doubtful that the Soviet Union would be
willing to act as Taiwan's supplier at the risk of further deteriorating
its relations with the PRC. Even if the Soviet Union were willing to
take such a risk, Taiwan would face serious difficulties in retraining
its pilots and maintenance personnel to use Soviet equipment.
Countries other than the United States and the Soviet Union are not in
a position to supply sophisticated weapons to Taiwan since they do
not want to offend the PRC.

The argument that the PRC is unlikely in the foreseeable future
to take military action against Taiwan for fear of jeopardizing its
developing relations with the United States and other Western
countries may be true today. However, the current circumstances
may change. As the Senate Foreign Relations Committee stated in its
Report on the Taiwan Enabling Act (later known as the Taiwan
Relations Act):

> Vice-Premier Teng is 74 years old and has twice been
> purged from office. Chinese foreign policy could again dra-
> matically change. A Sino-Soviet detente would free large
> numbers of Chinese troops currently near the Soviet border.
> The Chinese may miscalculate U.S. resolve to continue
> providing security to Taiwan. (S. Rep. No. 7, 96th Cong., 1st
> Sess. 11 (1979))

Furthermore, even without questioning the present political stability
in the PRC, we should note that the PRC has a record of changing
courses with bewildering speed. Only a few years ago, it was
accusing Japan of "militarism" and the United States of "imperialism." The rapid deterioration of relations between the PRC and
Vietnam and Albania is further evidence of the PRC's volatile foreign
policy.

In the Taiwan Relations Act of 1979, it is explicitly provided:

> It is the policy of the United States . . . to provide Taiwan
> with arms of a defensive character; and to maintain the
> capacity of the United States to resist any resort to force or
> other forms of coercion that would jeopardize the security,
> or the social or economic system, of the people on Taiwan.
> (22 U.S.C. § 3301 (Supp. III 1979))

If the Carter Administration and future U.S. administrations *sincerely* execute this Act by providing Taiwan with sufficient defensive weapons, Taiwan may be secure. However, the behavior of the Carter Administration indicates a propensity toward flattering the PRC at the expense of Taiwan, even in military sales and commercial matters.

For example, on March 29, 1979, both houses of the Congress passed the Taiwan Relations Act, but President Carter waited until the last day to sign the Act, *i.e.*, April 10. The President then waited for more than two months to issue an Executive Order on June 22 implementing the Act. The Order authorizes the Department of State to issue orders to grant privileges and immunities to Taiwan delegations in the U.S. However, more than four months have passed, and such orders have not yet been issued. The whole process seems to indicate that the Carter Administration intends to provide minimal execution and enforcement under the Act.

The second case relates to the termination of the U.S.-ROC Air Transport Agreement of December 20, 1946 (61 Stat. 2799; T.I.A.S. No. 1609), extended and amended on October 22, 1969 (T.I.A.S. No. 6773). At the time of normalization, the Carter Administration assured the Congress that except for the 1954 U.S.-ROC Mutual Defense Treaty, all other treaties with the ROC would be maintained. In his February 5, 1979 testimony before the Senate hearings on Taiwan, Deputy Secretary of State Warren Christopher said:

> First, we have moved to assure that with the exception of the mutual defense treaty and related agreements, our many treaties and other agreements with Taiwan—more than 55 in all—*will remain in force. (Taiwan: Hearings on S. 245 Before the Senate Comm. on Foreign Relations,* 96th Cong., 1st Sess. 15 (1979) (emphasis added))

Similarly, Senator Stone submitted the following question to the State Department for a written reply:

> Question 17. What specifically would the State Department plan to do, following "normalization" with the (a) FCN (Friendship, Commerce and Navigation Treaty of 1946), (b) Air Transport Agreement . . . ? (*Id.* at 77.)

The reply was:

> *All international agreements will remain in force,* except for the Mutual Defense Treaty and related agreements which will terminate on January 1, 1980. (*Id.* (emphasis added))

However, during Vice-President Mondale's visit to the PRC in August 1979, the Carter Administration announced that it had decided to terminate the 1946 Air Transport Agreement and to replace it with an "unofficial agreement." It also indicated that it would terminate some additional unspecified treaties or agreements with the ROC and to replace them with unofficial agreements.

The nightmare of the ROC people and government is that by continuing to downgrade its relations with Taiwan, the United States might implicitly invite the PRC to use force to take over Taiwan. Moreover, the Chinese people in Taiwan are afraid that one day the United States might collude with the PRC to press the ROC—by withholding arms sales or deliveries, curbing trade or other ties—to negotiate a "peaceful resolution" of the Taiwan question, which in Taiwan's view is nothing but the abandonment of 17 million Chinese people to totalitarian Communist rule.

A discussion of the future prospects of Taiwan cannot be complete without analyzing future ROC-PRC relations. For Taiwan to survive, it must not only maintain a sufficient defense force to make any PRC invasion unacceptably costly, but it must also avoid any action that could provoke the PRC to launch an attack. Any large-scale armed conflict in the Taiwan Strait, even one won by the ROC, would be costly to Taiwan. It is generally agreed that Taiwan could not survive a long-term sustained attack. Furthermore, because of Taiwan's heavy dependence on foreign trade (in 1978, Taiwan's worldwide exports comprised 48 percent, or $11 billion, of its gross national product) the ROC is very vulnerable to PRC interference. Even a paper blockade or an order requiring foreign shipping to Taiwan to get approval from Peking would greatly affect the economy of Taiwan. (For instance, export and import insurance cost would substantially increase.) For these reasons, it is essential for Taiwan to avoid any action that might provoke the PRC into military action or economic harassment to suffocate Taiwan.

At present, the PRC acknowledges that Taiwan has a higher standard of living. For that reason, the PRC no longer uses its former justification for invading Taiwan—to "liberate" the people of Taiwan from the "tyrannical rule of Chiang and U.S. imperialism." The PRC now appeals to the nationalistic feelings of the Chinese on Taiwan for a unified and strong China. Therefore, as long as eventual reunification of Taiwan with the Mainland is not foreclosed by some irrevocable actions by the authorities on Taiwan, pressure on PRC leaders to use force to settle the matter quickly will probably not be strong. It would therefore be unwise for Taiwan to declare itself the "Republic of Taiwan" rather than maintaining its present status as "the Republic of China" and its ultimate goal of unification with the Mainland.

If an independent Republic of Taiwan emerged and the PRC did not take swift military action to crush the new republic, then it might be gradually accepted by the international community as an independent state vis-a-vis China. This in turn would make it legally and politically more difficult for the PRC to reunite Taiwan with the Mainland in the future. Therefore, the emergence of an independent Taiwan Republic would most likely provoke the PRC to take prompt military action against Taiwan.

Moreover, in the future if the PRC develops a more stable leadership and more reasonable domestic and international policies, the ROC should try to develop a reasonable working relationship with the Mainland authorities through trade, technical and cultural exchanges, mutual visits and exchange of mails to let people on the Mainland know about the prosperous situation in Taiwan. An increase in the exchange of information would make it more difficult for the PRC authorities to mobilize public support for an invasion of Taiwan. If mutually beneficial working relations could be developed between the Mainland and Taiwan, the chances of a PRC invasion of the island would be markedly reduced.

In conclusion, my assessment of the future prospects of Taiwan is neither pessimistic nor optimistic because there are so many variable factors involved. Taiwan would have a bright future if:

(1) the ROC leadership is able to develop satisfactory programs to deal with those vital problems unrelated to U.S recognition and U.S.-PRC relations;

(2) the United States continues to supply *adequate* defensive weapons to the ROC and to treat Taiwan fairly in commercial, cultural and other relations;

(3) the democratization of the political process in Taiwan does not result in domestic turmoil, including the rise of the independence movement which would provoke intervention by the PRC; and

(4) a satisfactory working relation with the Mainland is developed in the future so as to reduce the possibility of PRC military intervention against Taiwan.

The United States, being the only country that can supply essential defensive weapons to Taiwan and being Taiwan's largest trading partner, investor and loan supplier, holds the key to the future of Taiwan. But this fact is also why Taiwan's future is unpredictable. Within the past year, we have seen secret and surprising negotiations result in a nearly complete reversal of 30 years of American policy toward China. Some commentators have viewed this reversal as a form of diplomatic public relations at a time when President Carter was trying to divert public attention from a Middle East stalemate; others have regarded it as an attempt to upstage the Nixon-Kissinger maneuvering at playing the China card against the Soviet Union; the great majority have decried the poor terms on which the shift in diplomatic recognition was negotiated. Regardless of the accuracy of these assessments, it is clear that the future of Taiwan is subject to the complex interplay of a vast array of unpredictable variables. With will power and fortitude, the United States can ensure the vitality of Taiwan. Lacking those qualities, the future of Taiwan will remain subject to the meanderings of an unsure American foreign policy.

In the last analysis, the future of Taiwan, to a substantial extent, lies in the hands of the American electorate choosing among the Presidential candidates. One can only hope that the American people will exercise their rights in a way that will ensure the freedom of the 17 million Chinese people in the Republic of China on Taiwan—a country which is the oldest United States ally in Asia and a people who share basic common values of individual freedom, free enterprise, and democracy with the American people.

B. **Statement of James C. Hsiung,** Professor of Politics, New York University

When he was awakened at 2:00 a.m. on December 16, 1978 (Taipei time) to be informed of President Carter's decision to derecognize the ROC, President Chiang Ching-kuo was presented with a fait accompli. He could only protest, but he could not reverse the policy. In view of Taiwan's economic dependency on the United States, he also could not take any retaliatory measures. Despite his initial insistence that the continuing relations must be on a "government-to-government" basis, Taiwan eventually had to accept what Washington insists are "unofficial" relations and the mythology that accompanies them.

What are Taiwan's options under the circumstances? Many scholars have suggested four possibilities.

Option 1: Negotiating with Peking. Vice-Premier Teng said to a visiting U.S. Senate delegation on January 9, 1979 that Taiwan could retain both its government and armed forces and remain fully autonomous after reunification with the Mainland, if Taiwan would cede its sovereignty. (*Peking Says Taiwan Can Keep Autonomy Under Unification,* New York Times, Jan. 10, 1979, at A1, col. 6.) While the offer may appear generous, the surrender of sovereignty would reduce Taiwan's juridical status to something approximating that of Tibet between 1949 and 1959. Premier Y.S. Sun in a televised address on January 11, 1979 flatly rejected Teng's proposal for achieving reunification through negotiation. (*Taiwan Premier Rebuffs Peking In its Proposal for Reunification,* New York Times, Jan. 12, 1979, at A4, col. 2.)

Leaders in Taiwan must have been aware that their outright rejection might have an adverse effect on some of Taiwan's sympathizers in the U.S. Premier Sun's prompt negative answer and his choice of a televised address to air it were calculated to ease the apprehensions of the island's 17 million population, especially the native Taiwanese. Most of these persons have only a very vague identification with the Mainland and are known to fear a sell-out by the KMT government to the PRC if negotiations should occur. There were even predictions about possible uprisings by the native Taiwanese should a sell-out be perceived as real and imminent. That possibility must have entered the minds of the ROC government leaders in rejecting a policy of negotiating with Peking.

Over the long haul, there is little likelihood for negotiation unless Peking can force Taiwan to come to participate, such as through the use of economic pressure. Although negotiation theorists in general believe that all disputes can settled by negotiation, it remains an elemental truth that no one will negotiate for his own extinction, even if it is extinction by installment.

Option 2: Declaring an independent Taiwan. Many supporters of Taiwan in the United States, including some in Congress, have suggested that Taiwan has no political future unless it carves out an independent existence in its own right. In the Shanghai Communique signed in 1972, the United States said that it did not challenge the claim that Taiwan was a part of China because that was the position held by both the people on the Mainland and on Taiwan. The implication is that should either the Taiwan Chinese or the mainland

Chinese change its view, the United States would not be bound by the one-China principle. In the normalization agreement, the United States reaffirmed the Shanghai Communique commitments and stopped just a hair's breadth short of accepting Peking's claim to Taiwan. Consequently, independence advocates assert that a declaration of independence making Taiwan a separate entity would not be totally inconsistent with the U.S. commitment to Peking under both the Shanghai Communique and the normalization agreement.

Attractive as the independence route may seem, I do not think it is a realistic course for Taiwan to pursue. In the first place, Taiwan's governmental structure is dominated by the Mainlanders, who have been in control of the "central government" since its evacuation to Taiwan in 1949. Their legitimacy depends in large measure on their avowed goal of recovering the lost Mainland, which in turn necessitates the perpetuation of the myth that there is "one-China." Declaration of an independent Taiwan would remove the right of the Mainlanders to rule Taiwan. In a world that increasingly accepts the principle of majority rule, the native Taiwanese, who make up 80 percent of the population, would then have the right to run the new government. Even if Chiang Ching-kuo were willing to accept such an arrangement, which I doubt, he would run into strong opposition from other members of the central government who would lose their positions. As long as the present Mainlander regime is in control, the independence route is probably out. I do not think that Chiang Ching-kuo has either the power or the courage to take this course.

Furthermore, the independence route is fraught with other dangers. Peking can tolerate Taiwan's continuing separate existence outside the "embrace of the motherland" only as long as the latter does not run away for good. The prospects of a perpetual secession would most likely compel Peking to intervene, even at great cost. Besides, as Taiwan's leaders sometimes confide in secret, there is no guarantee that a new independent Taiwan will be recognized by countries that have already switched recognition, including, and perhaps especially, the United States. These countries would be under the same pressures from Peking not to recognize the secessionist Taiwan that had prompted them to derecognize Taiwan in the first place.

Finally, although sentiments are strong among native Taiwanese for an independent existence detached from the China legend, there is no one group that speaks for all the natives. Dissidents within the island and abroad are united only in their varying degrees of dissatisfaction with the Mainlander regime. Prospects of forming a unified succession regime are extremely slim. My own estimate is that if the existing KMT regime collapses under internal and external pressures, the outcome would be far worse than what followed the departure of Shah Reza Pahlevi in Iran. I see no group approximating the diehards rallying around Ayatollah Khomeini which could put together a stable new government. Any prolonged internal turmoil would invite Peking's intervention.

Option 3: The nuclear option. The most devastating effect of normalization is the uncertainty created regarding Taiwan's future security. The announced termination of the mutual security treaty after December 31, 1979, has generated greater apprehensions in Taiwan than the act of derecognition itself. Although U.S. arms sales were originally said to be not affected by the "China deal," the subsequent announcement by Washington about a one-year moratorium on new purchases for 1979 has reinforced the Taiwan people's fear about their security.

Many who are concerned with protecting Taiwan from an outside threat have suggested that Taiwan should develop an independent nuclear arsenal. But Taiwan lacks the necessary fissionable material. Three times in the past, so far as I know, the ROC government attempted to obtain enriched uranium from outside suppliers. U.S. intervention prevented the consummation of the deal each time. Taiwan remains totally dependent on the United States for the supply of enriched uranium for its nuclear power plants, which will be supplying over one-third of the island's electric power by the year 1985. The United States will cut off its uranium supplies to Taiwan should any of the enriched uranium be diverted to the manufacture of nuclear weapons.

Aside from the supply problem, I am not sure if the nuclear idea will necessarily make Taiwan safer vis-a-vis a much stronger nuclear power on the other side of the Strait. The island will be extremely vulnerable during the interim before it acquires a credible deterrent force. A serious attempt to go nuclear without U.S. backing—even assuming that was possible—may trigger a Chinese impulse to strike the island's nascent program.

Option 4: Playing the Soviet card. If Carter plays the China card, it has been asked, couldn't Taiwan play the Soviet card? My question is: Is there a Soviet card for Taiwan to play? The KMT had a nightmarish past relationship with the Soviet Union during 1923-1949 and is still living with the memory. Leaders in Taiwan today are aware of the peril of "inviting the bear into the house." A serious flirtation with Moscow could so displease the United States that it might bring sanctions that Taiwan can ill afford. In the past, Taiwan was more than once forced by Washington to declare in public that it would not flirt with the Soviet Union. There is no evidence that the U.S. concern has abated in the new circumstances. Furthermore, any contact by Taiwan that goes beyond casual trade and possibly purchase of strategic goods and services from Moscow may provoke a reaction from Peking that may outweigh any advantage gained from a Soviet connection.

I do not rule out the possibility that if sufficiently desperate, and faced with imminent danger, Taiwan might grasp at the last straw. But in such an event, probably no amount of Soviet aid would reverse Taiwan's fate. Moreover, Taiwan simply cannot afford to lose United States support, or to provoke Peking into any drastic action. Drifting too close to the Soviet orbit would produce both of these consequences. The Soviet Union also knows that a relationship with Taiwan would ruin any possibility of making up with Peking again. My answer to the rhetorical question raised above is that there is probably no Soviet card for Taiwan to play, although very casual contacts with low political coloration, such as trade conducted through Eastern Europe, should not be ruled out.

All the above options are not real options. The only likely course of action open to Taiwan, as I see it, is to attempt to keep itself afloat and to maintain the status quo *creatively*.

In foreign affairs, Taiwan at a minimum must maintain and, if possible, upgrade its commercial and cultural relations with the United States. It also must endeavor to preserve the existing diplomatic relations with the 20 or so countries that still recognize the ROC. Without doubt, Taiwan's survival depends upon its ability to maintain its foreign trade and to thwart any attempt by Peking to strangle it economically.

"Creative Pluralism"

These minimal goals may require Taiwan to adopt a foreign policy of "creative pluralism" with both economic and political connotations. External economic pluralism means, first of all, diversifying Taiwan's trading partners—cutting across ideological lines more freely than ever before. Despite official denials, Taiwan goods are known to have found their way to the East European market, at least since the ROC's expulsion from the United Nations in 1971. The game of survival may force Taiwan to extend its trade to the Soviet market, Moscow willing. Many Taiwan businessmen I know are not hesitant to admit that they are waiting for the government to give the go-ahead.

In the past, Taiwan's government was bent on impressing the American public with its commitment to "free enterprise." The political propaganda pay-offs are obvious. But the upshot was that the island's industries developed pretty much on their own. Medium and small industries were left to their own devices to fight for a share of the outside market, often against much larger competitors, including enterprises supported by the South Korean government. Along with bureaucratic inertia, the "free enterprise" millstone largely explains why the Taiwan government stopped short of copying South Korea's state mercantilism, which has served that country so well. United States derecognition may necessitate the introduction of greater state involvement in consolidating the island's medium and small industries' assault on the external market.

Another reason for the government's "shyness" about greater state patronage has to do with an unspoken agreement between the Mainlander-dominant government and the native Taiwanese industrialists: The Mainlanders had ultimate control over politics, but the Taiwan natives would be given a more or less free hand in economics. This deal has helped hold Taiwan together by balancing political power with economic power. But the old balancing game at home may have to change in order to accommodate the dictates of survival.

Taiwan's survival depends on its ability to continue its *separate existence* as a de facto sovereign entity. Earlier I argued against the practicality of an independent Taiwan state. The status quo of a separate existence, however, is very likely to last for the forseeable future. This is fact, not analysis. Short of explicitly declaring independence, the Taiwan government could cease its assertions about representing all China. Instead, it could present itself as representing the people in the territories under its effective jurisdiction, and invite all foreign governments to recognize it as no more than just that. This curtailment of the Taiwan government's position would have the effect of suspending its claims to, hence legal ties with, the rest of China, but would not constitute a permanent breakaway in the juridical sense. The concept of "one-China" would remain a goal for the future. The choice of foreign countries would be to decide whether or not to recognize a "simple reality" as long as Taiwan leads a de facto separate existence.

Political "creative pluralism" has both its international and domestic application. Internationally, it means that Taiwan must be able to sell the simple reality of its de facto separate existence to as many states as are willing to accept it. "Pluralism" implies a theory of multiple recognition, built on a distinction between legal claims and de facto reality. "Creative" denotes that the world must come to grips with a temporal dimension in the China/Taiwan equation. While the notion of "one-China" lives on, the fact is that there is a temporal interregnum between the present when a separate Taiwan exists, and the time when Taiwan becomes fully integrated with the Mainland. The duration of the time gap will depend on many factors, including the island's economic performance and military might. But, more important, it will depend on internal stability.

Giving up its claims to the Mainland is necessary for Taiwan to gain recognition as a separate sovereign entity *ad interim*. But the very same renunciation of those pretensions immediately calls into question the present Taipei government's right to rule. There will be no need for the dual system of a "central" government on top of a provincial government. There will be no justification for why the Mainlander minority must rule over the Taiwanese majority. In anticipation of this consequence, the foreign policy of "creative pluralism" dictates a domestic addendum, which is that the internal power balance must shift. The KMT government must take more than half-hearted steps to effectuate the smooth transition of power to the hands of more Taiwanese leaders. Any power transfer is painful. But for the sake of Taiwan's internal stability and external survival, there is no other choice. The KMT would be acting wisely if it starts the transition while it still has the power and a good bargaining position. Defensive power sharing will pay off for the KMT in the long run. If it refuses now, there may be nothing to salvage later. In the midst of the infighting, Taiwan's own external security may even be compromised.

The power shift, along with the international "redressing" of Taiwan mentioned above, must be accompanied by a massive reeducation effort across the island. Instead of the myth of recovering the lost Mainland, the new political education will have to stress Taiwan's own identity under the existing circumstances, the need for ethnic unity, a blurring of the Mainlander and Taiwanese distinction, and the cardinal rules of the game of survival by which every Taiwan resident must abide. Legitimacy of the future Taiwan government, ruled by both Taiwanese and Mainlanders, will depend on its ability to hold the island together as a separate sovereign entity, and to win support from the outside world.

I am not so certain that what I have just suggested will happen. Nor am I certain that the leadership surrounding Chiang Ching-kuo will have the freedom and the determination to come forward and declare a suspension of the ROC's claims to all of China, and to project unequivocally the image of a de facto sovereign entity while awaiting the millenium of national reunification.

What will be the shape of that future for Taiwan? The answer will depend on: (a) the resolve and adroitness with which Taiwan will pursue what I have called a policy of "creative pluralism"; (b) the viability of the island's economy, especially its international trade; and (c) the successful transfer of power, over a reasonable period of time, to the hands of more Taiwanese leaders. A great deal will also depend on the future state of U.S. relations with the PRC, and on the attitudes and policy of Jimmy Carter's successors in the White House. Finally, the future of Taiwan will depend in large measure on its own strength vis-a-vis that of mainland China.

If I have sounded too "iffy," it is precisely because we are dealing with a very "iffy" situation for which no crystal ball, no matter how sophisticated, is equipped to offer a more definite answer. Offering one's own wishes, whims, or polemics is one thing. Offering an objective assessment is a totally different matter. I am too proud of my professional reputation and too concerned with my personal integrity to do less than give an objective assessment as I see it now.

C. Statement of Wei-ming Tu, Professor of History, University of California, Berkeley

As a concerned Chinese-American born in Kunming, China, raised in Taiwan fifth grade through college, who became a U.S. citizen in 1976, I would like to offer some of my views on the conflicting perspectives expressed by the participants to the "dialogue" of the preceding chapters. I cannot, frankly speaking, present my thoughts on the issue as a detached analyst. Like all of the participants, I also have an intense personal interest in the issue. My opinions are necessarily shaped by my own limited understanding of the complex phenomenon, my hopes for a peaceful solution to the "unification problem," and my commitment to a better livelihood for the Chinese people as a whole.

The Rhetorical Situation. The very fact that the above dialogue has actually taken place is exceedingly significant. Of course, it is not at all unusual to talk with people holding a variety of strong views on the Taiwan issue. Indeed, the future of Taiwan weighs so heavily on the conscience and consciousness of all concerned Chinese that a discussion of this topic, even among a small coterie of like-minded friends, often generates heated emotional arguments. As a result, the Chinese community in America has been seriously polarized and fragmented into pro-PRC, pro-ROC, and pro-Independence groups. These groups rarely talk to each other, and have their own organizations, activities, and audiences. They symbolize not only three different political positions, but also three divergent worlds of discourse, among which there is no true dialogue. Consequently, it is, to say the least, unusual for people advocating radically dissimilar views to agree to meet in the same conference room.

In fact, at present a dialogue among concerned Chinese on the future of Taiwan cannot take place in Taipei or in Peking. The overwhelming majority of the Chinese people on both sides of the Taiwan Strait are not even aware of the various intellectual and practical options explored in this volume. The few who know lack the freedom to articulate their views. Ironically, pro-ROC magazines and newspapers published in Hong Kong such as *Ming-pao yueh-k'an* and *Chung-kuo jen* are not allowed into Taiwan, and pro-PRC publications from abroad such as *Ch'i-shih nien-tai* cannot be circulated on the Mainland. The possibility of exploring vital issues is much wider in Hong Kong, but its physical and psychological proximity to the PRC distorts the environment for candid discussions. The United States is one of the few places where an open dialogue among concerned Chinese is still possible.

An Historical Note. The status of Taiwan as an integral part of the Chinese civilization-state was never questioned prior to the 17th century. Dutch traders established fortified posts on the "beautiful island" of Formosa (as the Portuguese had named it) in 1624. The Dutch were ousted in 1661 by the Ming loyalist Cheng Ch'eng-kung (Koxinga). His supporters held the island for more than two decades against the newly established Ch'ing dynasty. The Ch'ing forces finally conquered Taiwan in 1683 and Emperor K'ang-hsi incorporated it into Fukien province. However, the Ch'ing government was preoccupied with the defense of the Inner Asian border in the northwest, and neglected the development of a strong navy. As a result, the coasts of Kuangtung, Fukien and Chekiang were often dominated by pirates in the 18th century. It may not be farfetched to suggest that for the next several decades Taiwan was under the sphere of influence of pirate leaders. While the Ch'ing claimed sovereignty over Taiwan, it is undeniable that for many years the main actors in Taiwan were Chinese from the coastal area. For example, some of the most devastating rebellions in Taiwan of the 1780s seem to have been instigated by the secret Triad Society of South China.

Taiwan was opened to the Western powers as a treaty port in the 1860s. The Japanese government sent a punitive force of more than 3,000 soldiers against Taiwan in 1874 on the ground that 54 shipwrecked merchants from Ryukyu had been massacred by Taiwanese aborigines. In 1895 the Treaty of Shimonoseki obliged China to cede Taiwan to Japan. After 50 years of Japanese rule, Taiwan was returned to China at the conclusion of the Second World War. Since 1949 it has been under the control of the Nationalist government.

Conflicting Perspectives. Anyone familiar with modern Chinese history since the Opium War of 1840 easily understands why the PRC and the ROC both insist, as a matter of principle, that Taiwan is an integral part of China. The appeal to nationalistic sentiments is deeply rooted in history. Surely it is conceivable that after 80 years of actual separation from the Mainland, Taiwan has become a de facto independent political entity. But it is difficult to maintain that Taiwan is not Chinese ethnically, linguistically, and culturally. To say that "I am a Taiwanese, not a Chinese" is therefore a political statement. It is a political protest—a deliberate attempt to sever one's ethnic, linguistic, and cultural ties with China.

One need not be radically anti-Chinese, however, to assert a preference for de facto or de jure political independence. While the ROC denies any intention of moving toward either an independent Taiwan or a "two-China" stance, its current policy is to seriously explore the possibility of becoming a new intermediate entity, "China-Taiwan," often expressed as Republic of China on Taiwan, ROC on Taiwan, Chinese Republic on Taiwan, or Chinese Government at Taipei (as opposed to Chinese Government at Peking). With a stretch of imagination, the ROC may not even object to the idea of

Chung-hua Taiwan kung-ho-kuo (The Chinese Republic of Taiwan), if it can keep the flag, the national anthem, and the status of de facto independence.

The position of the PRC is less ambivalent: Taiwan can keep its military defense, foreign relations, economic status, social system, and governmental organization for the time being, but it must recognize its role as a "province" of China and it must not refuse indefinitely to negotiate. Mutual trade, correspondence, and travel arrangements between the Mainland and Taiwan are proposed as concrete steps toward the eventual goal of "unification." Yet, Peking has not specified the actual manner of unification. Hong Kong, Macao, and Tibet have been mentioned as possible models. The use of force is not ruled out. Recently there are indications that the model of "special area" (*t'e-ch'u*), comparable to the relationship of the Communist-occupied territories of North China to Chungking during the Sino-Japanese War, is also being considered. The immediate demand then will be a symbolic one, namely that the PRC flag must be flown on Taiwan.

Some concerned Chinese abroad, intent on finding a permanent solution to the delicate issue, propose a kind of "Chinese Confederation" or "Chinese Commonwealth" as a framework which would include not only the island-state of Taiwan but also the city-state of Singapore and the colony of Hong Kong. The idea is predicated on the belief (some would say wishful thinking) that in the long run a peaceful and dynamic interaction between Maritime China and Continental China will be beneficial to all parties concerned.

Shared Concerns. Even the most militant proponents for a radical restructuring of the status quo in Taiwan share the view that the well-being not only of the 17 million people on the island but also of the 960 million Chinese on the Mainland will best be served by a non-violent transformation. It is inevitable that the political system in Taiwan will undergo a fundamental change in the next few years, either by choice or by default. Hopefully, the emerging leadership will realistically appraise the current situation with a holistic view toward the future. If so, it is likely that (1) the verbal aggressiveness toward the PRC will be significantly reduced; (2) the political power base will be greatly enlarged through democratic elections; (3) foreign trade will be further diversified; (4) non-official contacts with the PRC will be increased; and (5) an interim solution to unification will be found.

Appendix 3

The Shanghai Communique, Department of State Bulletin, vol. 66, no. 1708, pp. 435-38 (Mar. 20, 1972)

President Richard Nixon of the United States of America visited the People's Republic of China at the invitation of Premier Chou En-lai of the People's Republic of China from February 21 to February 28, 1972. Accompanying the President were Mrs. Nixon, U.S. Secretary of State William Rogers, Assistant to the President Dr. Henry Kissinger, and other American officials.

President Nixon met with Chairman Mao Tse-tung of the Communist Party of China on February 21. The two leaders had a serious and frank exchange of views on Sino-U.S. relations and world affairs.

During the visit, extensive, earnest and frank discussions were held between President Nixon and Premier Chou En-lai on the normalization of relations between the United States of America and the People's Republic of China, as well as on other matters of interest to both sides. In addition, Secretary of State William Rogers and Foreign Minister Chi Peng-fei held talks in the same spirit.

President Nixon and his party visited Peking and viewed cultural, industrial and agricultural sites, and they also toured Hangchow and Shanghai where, continuing discussions with Chinese leaders, they viewed similar places of interest.

The leaders of the People's Republic of China and the United States of America found it beneficial to have this opportunity, after so many years without contact, to present candidly to one another their views on a variety of issues. They reviewed the international situation in which important changes and great upheavals are taking place and expounded their respective positions and attitudes.

The U.S. side stated: Peace in Asia and peace in the world requires efforts both to reduce immediate tensions and to eliminate the basic causes of conflict. The United States will work for a just and secure peace: just, because it fulfills the aspirations of peoples and nations for freedom and progress; secure, because it removes the danger of foreign aggression. The United States supports individual freedom and social progress for all the peoples of the world, free of outside pressure or intervention. The United States believes that the effort to reduce tensions is served by improving communication between countries that have different ideologies so as to lessen the risks of confrontation through accident, miscalculation or misunderstanding. Countries should treat each other with mutual respect and be willing to compete peacefully, letting performance be the ultimate judge. No country should claim infallibility and each country should be prepared to re-examine its own attitudes for the common good. The United States stressed that the peoples of Indochina should be allowed to determine their destiny without outside intervention; its constant primary objective has been a negotiated solution; the eight-point proposal put forward by the Republic of Vietnam and the United States on January 27, 1972 represents a basis for the attainment of that objective; in the absence of a negotiated settlement the United States envisages the ultimate withdrawal of all U.S. forces from the region consistent with the aim of self-determination for each country of Indochina. The United States will maintain its close ties with and support for the Republic of Korea; the United States will support efforts of the Republic of Korea to seek a relaxation of tension and increased communication in the Korean peninsula. The United States places the highest value on its friendly relations with Japan; it will continue to develop the existing close bonds. Consistent with the United Nations Security Council Resolution of December 21, 1971, the United States favors the continuation of the ceasefire between India and Pakistan and the withdrawal of all military forces to within their own territories and to their own sides of the ceasefire line in Jammu and Kashmir; the United States supports the right of the peoples of South Asia to shape their own future in peace, free of military threat, and without having the area become the subject of great power rivalry.

The Chinese side stated. Wherever there is oppression, there is resistance. Countries want independence, nations want liberation and the people want revolution—this has become the irresistible trend of history. All nations, big or small, should be equal; big nations should not bully the small and strong nations should not bully the weak. China will never be a superpower and it opposes hegemony and power politics of any kind. The Chinese side stated that it firmly supports the struggles of all the oppressed people and nations for freedom and liberation and that the people of all countries have the right to choose their social systems according to their own wishes and the right to safeguard the independence, sovereignty and territorial integrity of their own countries and oppose foreign aggression, interference, control and subversion. All foreign troops should be withdrawn to their own countries.

The Chinese side expressed its firm support to the peoples of Vietnam, Laos and Cambodia in their efforts for the attainment of their goal and its firm support to the seven-point proposal of the Provisional Revolutionary Government of the Republic of South Vietnam and the elaboration of February this year on the two key problems in the proposal, and to the Joint Declaration of the Summit Conference of the Indochinese Peoples. It firmly supports the eight-point program for the peaceful unification of Korea put forward by the Government of the Democratic People's Republic of Korea on April 12, 1971, and the stand for the abolition of the "U.N. Commission for the Unification and Rehabilitation of Korea." It firmly opposes the revival and outward expansion of Japanese militarism and firmly supports the Japanese's desire to build an independent, democratic, peaceful and neutral Japan. It firmly maintains that India and Pakistan should, in accordance with United Nations resolutions on the India-Pakistan question, immediately withdraw all their forces to their respective territories and to their own sides of the ceasefire line in Jammu and Kashmir and firmly supports the Pakistan Government and people in their struggle to preserve their independence and sovereignty and the people of Jammu and Kashmir in their struggle for the right of self-determination.

There are essential differences between China and the United States in their social systems and foreign policies. However, the two sides agreed that countries, regardless of their systems, should conduct their relations on the principles of respect for the sovereignty and territorial integrity of all states, non-aggression against other states, noninterference in the internal affairs of other states, equality and mutual benefit, and peaceful coexistence. International disputes should be settled on this basis, without resorting to the use or threat of force. The United States and the People's Republic of China are prepared to apply these principles to their mutual relations.

With these principles of international relations in mind the two sides stated that:

Progress toward the normalization of relations between China and the United States is in the interests of all countries;

Both wish to reduce the danger of international military conflict;

Neither should seek hegemony in the Asia-Pacific region and each is opposed to efforts by any other country or group of countries to establish such hegemony; and

Neither is prepared to negotiate on behalf of any third party or to enter into agreements or understandings with the other directed at other states.

Both sides are of the view that it would be against the interests of the peoples of the world for any major country to collude with another against other countries, or for major countries to divide up the world into spheres of interest.

The two sides reviewed the long-standing serious disputes between China and the United States. The Chinese side reaffirmed its position: The Taiwan question is the crucial question obstructing the normalization of relations between China and the United States; the Government of the People's Republic of China is the sole legal government of China; Taiwan is a province of China which has long been returned to the motherland; the liberation of Taiwan is China's internal affair in which no other country has the right to interfere; and all U.S. forces and military installations must be withdrawn from Taiwan. The Chinese Government firmly opposes any activities which aim at the creation of "one China, one Taiwan," "one China, two governments," "two Chinas," and "Independent Taiwan" or advocate that "the status of Taiwan remains to be determined."

The U.S. side declared: The United States acknowledges that all Chinese on either side of the Taiwan Strait maintain there is but one China and that Taiwan is a part of China. The United States Government does not challenge that position. It reaffirms its interest in a peaceful settlement of the Taiwan question by the Chinese themselves. With this prospect in mind, it affirms the ultimate objective of the withdrawal of all U.S. forces and military installations from Taiwan. In the meantime, it will progressively reduce its forces and military installations on Taiwan as the tension in the area diminishes.

The two sides agreed that it is desirable to broaden the understanding between the two peoples. To this end, they discussed specific areas in such fields as science, technology, culture, sports and journalism, in which people-to-people contacts and exchanges would be mutually beneficial. Each side undertakes to facilitate the further development of such contacts and exchanges.

Both sides view bilateral trade as another area from which mutual benefit can be derived, and agreed that economic relations based on equality and mutual benefit are in the interest of the peoples of the two countries. They agree to facilitate the progressive development of trade between their two countries.

The two sides agreed that they will stay in contact through various channels, including the sending of a Senior U.S. representative to Peking from time to time for concrete consultations to further the normalization of relations between the two countries and continue to exchange views on issues of common interest.

The two sides expressed the hope that the gains achieved during this visit would open up new prospects for the relations between the two countries. They believe that the normalization of relations between the two countries is not only in the interest of the Chinese and American peoples but also contributes to the relaxation of tension in Asia and the world.

President Nixon, Mrs. Nixon and the American party expressed their appreciation for the gracious hospitality shown them by the Government and people of the People's Republic of China.

Appendix 4

Remarks of President Carter on Establishment of Diplomatic Relations Between the United States of America and the People's Republic of China, December 15, 1978 (White House press release)

Good evening.

I would like to read a joint communique which is being simultaneously issued in Peking at this very moment by the leaders of the People's Republic of China:

> Joint Communique on the Establishment of Diplomatic Relations Between the United States of America and the People's Republic of China, January 1, 1979

> The United States of America and the People's Republic of China have agreed to recognize each other and to establish diplomatic relations as of January 1st, 1979.

> The United States recognizes the Government of the People's Republic of China as the sole legal government of China. Within this context, the people of the United States will maintain cultural, commercial and other unofficial relations with the people of Taiwan.

> The United States of America and the People's Republic of China reaffirm the principles agreed on by the two sides in the Shanghai Communique of 1972 and emphasize once again that:

> —Both sides wish to reduce the danger of international military conflict.

—Neither should seek hegemony—that is a dominance of one nation over the other—in the Asia-Pacific region or in any other region of the world and each is opposed to efforts by any other country or group of countries to establish such hegemony.

—Neither is prepared to negotiate on behalf of any other third party or to enter into agreements or understandings with the other directed at other states.

—The Government of the United States of America acknowledges the Chinese position that there is but one China and Taiwan is part of China.

—Both believe that normalization of Sino-American relations is not only in the interest of the Chinese and American peoples but also contributes to the cause of peace in Asia and in the world.

—The United States of America and the People's Republic of China will exchange Ambassadors and establish embassies on March 1, 1979.

Yesterday, our country and the People's Republic of China reached this final historic agreement.

On January 1, 1979, a little more than two weeks from now, our two governments will implement full normalization of diplomatic relations.

As a nation of gifted people who comprise about one-fourth of the total population of the earth, China plays, already, an important role in world affairs—a role that can only grow more important in the years ahead.

We do not undertake this important step for transient tactical or expedient reasons. In recognizing the People's Republic of China, that it is the single government of China, we are recognizing simple reality. But far more is involved in this decision that just recognition of a fact.

Before the estrangement of recent decades, the American and the Chinese people had a long history of friendship. We have already begun to rebuild some of those previous ties. Now, our rapidly expanding relationship requires the kind of structure that only full diplomatic relations will make possible.

The change that I am announcing tonight will be of great long-term benefit to the peoples of both our country and China—and, I believe, to all the peoples of the world.

Normalization—and the expanded commercial and cultural relations that it will bring—will contribute to the well-being of our own Nation, to our own national interest, and it will also enhance the stability of Asia.

These more positive relations with China can beneficially affect the world in which we live and the world in which our children will live.

We have already begun to inform our allies and other nations and the Members of the Congress of the details of our intended action. But I wish also tonight to convey a special message to the people of Taiwan—I have already communicated with the leaders in Taiwan—with whom the American people have had and will have extensive, close and friendly relations.

This is important between our two peoples.

As the United States asserted in the Shanghai Communique of 1972, issued on President Nixon's historic visit, we will continue to have an interest in the peaceful resolution of the Taiwan issue.

I have paid special attention to ensuring that normalization of relations between our country and the People's Republic will not jeopardize the well-being of the people of Taiwan.

The people of our country will maintain our current commercial, cultural, trade and other relations with Taiwan through nongovernmental means. Many other countries in the world are already successfully doing this.

These decisions and these actions open a new and important chapter in our country's history, and also in world affairs.

To strengthen and to expedite the benefits of this new relationship between China and the United States, I am pleased to announce that Vice Premier Teng has accepted my invitation and will visit Washington at the end of January. His visit will give our governments the opportunity to consult with each other on global issues and to begin working together to enhance the cause of world peace.

These events are the final result of long and serious negotiations begun by President Nixon in 1972, and continued under the leadership of President Ford. The results bear witness to the steady, determined and bipartisan effort of our country to build a world in which peace will be the goal and the responsibility of all nations.

The normalization of relations between the United States and China has no other purpose than this—the advancement of peace.

It is in this spirit, at this season of peace, that I take special pride in sharing this good news with you tonight.

Appendix 5

United States Statement Accompanying the Joint Communique,
December 15, 1978, Department of State Bulletin, vol. 79, no. 2022,
p. 26 (Jan. 1979)

As of January 1, 1979, the United States of America recognizes
the People's Republic of China as the sole legal Government of
China. On the same date, the People's Republic of China accords similar recognition to the United States of America. The United States
thereby establishes diplomatic relations with the People's Republic of
China.

On that same date, January 1, 1979, the United States of
America will notify Taiwan that it is terminating diplomatic relations
and that the mutual defence treaty between the United States and the
Republic of China is being terminated in accordance with the
provisions of the treaty. The United States also states that it will be
withdrawing its remaining military personnel from Taiwan within
four months.

In the future, the American people and the people of Taiwan will
maintain commercial, cultural, and other relations without official
government representation and without diplomatic relations.

The administration will seek adjustments to our laws and regulations to permit the maintenance of commercial, cultural, and other
non-governmental relationships in the new circumstances that will
exist after normalization.

The United States is confident that the people of Taiwan face a
peaceful and prosperous future. The United States continues to have

an interest in the peaceful resolution of the Taiwan issue and expects that the Taiwan issue will be settled peacefully by the Chinese themselves.

The United States believes that the establishment of diplomatic relations with the People's Republic will contribute to the welfare of the American people, to the stability of Asia where the United States has major security and economic interest, and to the peace of the entire world.

Appendix 6

Statement of the Chinese Government, Peking Review, no. 51, pp. 8-9 (Dec. 22, 1978)

The Government of the People's Republic of China on December 16 issued a statement on the establishment of diplomatic relations between China and the United States.

The full text of the statement reads as follows:

Statement of the Government of the People's Republic of China

As of January 1, 1979, the People's Republic of China and the United States of America recognize each other and establish diplomatic relations, thereby ending the prolonged abnormal relationship between them. This is a historic event in Sino-U.S. relations.

As is known to all, the Government of the People's Republic of China is the sole legal Government of China and Taiwan is a part of China. The question of Taiwan was the crucial issue obstructing the normalization of relations between China and the United States. It has now been resolved between the two countries in the spirit of the Shanghai Communique and through their joint efforts, thus enabling the normalization of relations so ardently desired by the people of the two countries. As for the way of bringing Taiwan back to the embrace of the motherland and reunifying the country, it is entirely China's internal affair.

At the invitation of the U.S. Government, Teng Hsiao-ping, Vice-Premier of the State Council of the People's Republic of China, will pay an official visit to the United States in January 1979, with a view to further promoting the friendship between the two peoples and good relations between the countries.

Appendix 7

Speech by Secretary of State Cyrus Vance, January 15, 1979,
"Stability in East Asia: The U.S. Role," Senate Committee on
Foreign Relations, 96th Cong., 1st Sess., Sino-American Relations: A
New Turn 62-67 (Comm. Print 1979)

I am delighted that so many of you have joined us today. I
particularly want to thank the two main business organizations
represented here, and especially their leadership, for their efforts in
advancing public understanding of a major foreign policy issue. Both
Councils have played—and will continue to play—important roles in
strengthening our economic relations.

It is now one month since the President announced that the
United States and the People's Republic of China had reached
agreement on the establishment of full and normal diplomatic
relations. Today I would like to share with you some of the background leading up to the President's historic decision, and outline
what we believe it means for the United States and for the world.

Few other foreign policy issues have so long divided Americans
as The China Question. In the 1930's, Americans became deeply
aware and often passionately concerned with the tragedy and suffering of China. In the early 1940's, our two nations fought together
against the Axis powers. In the late 1940's we tried, ultimately
without success, to help the two sides in the Chinese civil war find a
peaceful settlement to their conflict.

Relations between the People's Republic of China and the United
States reached a nadir in the 1950's. Our armies clashed in Korea,
and at home the China issue left a deep mark on the domestic political

landscape. One of the tragedies of that period was the destruction of the careers of some outstanding Foreign Service officers because they reported events in Asia as they saw them.

The impasse in our relations with Peking persisted despite the emergence during the 1960's of incontestable evidence of serious rivalry between the Soviet Union and China. The United States, enmeshed in military involvement in Southeast Asia, and China, preoccupied with the Cultural Revolution, were unable to make progress towards overcoming our differences.

1971 marked the beginning of a new phase. Across a vast gulf of misunderstanding and mutual distrust, the governments of Peking and the United States began a dialogue, starting with Henry Kissinger's dramatic trip to Peking in 1971 and President Nixon's visit in 1972. The Shanghai Communique of that year set a framework for our new relationship.

But that dialogue was incomplete. The United States still formally recognized the Republic of China—whose de facto control encompassed only Taiwan and a few adjacent islands—as the legal government of China. Despite this, we were able to begin contacts and ultimately, in 1973, even establish Liaison Offices in Washington and Peking. But the nature of the relationship with Peking remained limited in scope and depth by the political, legal, and economic implications of our lack of mutual recognition.

Non-recognition—the delicate state in which we dealt with Peking in the six years after the Shanghai Communique—presented daily practical problems. Although both sides made major efforts to minimize these limitations, they became increasingly inhibiting. Discussions with the Chinese often foundered on the fact that in the absence of recognition, many activities either could not proceed at all or had to be conducted at a low level. Contacts were constrained, including those that might have produced greater understanding on global issues. Trade was limited, and opportunities often would go elsewhere. Legal problems hung over commercial transactions because of American claims and frozen PRC assets dating back to 1950. More importantly, not to try to move forward would have been to risk moving backward—and backward movement in U.S.-Chinese relations would have caused serious damage to our global position.

So even before he was inaugurated, President Carter made his first China decision. In an act of continuity with two previous Presidents, he reaffirmed the Shanghai Communique as the basis for our relationship, and specifically reaffirmed its commitment to work towards normal relations.

We were not at all certain at that time that we could indeed reach that ultimate goal. But we felt it essential to try, and we were prepared to take as much time as was necessary to achieve it on an acceptable basis.

With this in mind, we began discussions within the Administration, as well as an intensive series of consultations both with Members of Congress and with a wide cross-section of American businessmen, scholars, and others. From our consultations and review, two central thrusts, and several specific concerns, emerged.

These basic thrusts could not have been clearer: on the one hand, a substantial majority of Americans wished to see the United States and the People's Republic of China establish diplomatic relations; but at the same time, an equally large majority had deep concerns about Taiwan's future prosperity, security, and stability. We shared these concerns. The President decided that we would only establish diplomatic relations with Peking if such an action could be accomplished in a way that did not damage the well-being of the people on Taiwan or reduce the chances for a peaceful settlement of the Taiwan question by the Chinese themselves.

Beyond these basic considerations, several specific concerns emerged. First, there was widespread and legitimate concern over Peking's insistence that prior to normalization the United States must unilaterally abrogate the Mutual Defense Treaty with Taiwan, rather than terminate it in accordance with its own provisions, to which the United States and Taiwan had agreed in 1954. Furthermore, we wished to establish that after normalization, even in the absence of diplomatic relations with Taiwan, all other agreements and treaties would remain in effect.

Second, we shared with Congress and the American public a deep concern over the strong assertions by Chinese officials concerning their right to "liberate" Taiwan in any way they saw fit. From an American point of view, the peaceful settlement of the Taiwan issue by the Chinese themselves was of critical importance; we could not move forward if Peking continued to talk and think about the Taiwan issue in such inflammatory terms.

Third, a consensus rapidly emerged, inside and outside the government, that it was essential that we continue a wide range of relations with the people on Taiwan on a nongovernmental basis after normalization. In particular, these post-normalization relations would have to include continued sale of defensive weapons to Taiwan.

With these priorities emerging, I visited Peking in August of 1977, and Dr. Brzezinski went there in May of 1978. We found a newly confident leadership emerging in Peking as a period of intense internal turmoil subsided. We found many points of common interest on global matters, although on some important issues we continued to have differences. Our discussions on normalization were of an exploratory nature. These overall discussions reinforced our view that a strong, secure and peaceful China was in the interest of world peace.

In the early summer, President Carter instructed Ambassador Leonard Woodcock, Chief of the Liaison Office in Peking, to begin a series of presentations outlining our views on normalization. In five meetings, Ambassador Woodcock laid out the American position.

On September 19, President Carter met with the new head of the Chinese Liaison Office in Washington, Ambassador Chai Zemin. Involving himself directly in the discussions for the first time, the President told the Chinese that we were ready to normalize relations if our concerns about the future well-being of the people on Taiwan were met.

In completing his presentations on November 4, Ambassador Woodcock indicated to the Chinese that we would be willing to work toward a January 1, 1979, target date for normalization if our concerns were met. The Chinese began their response in early December. In mid-December, negotiations intensified with Vice Premier Deng Xiaoping becoming personally involved. Finally, on December 14, we reached agreement that met our fundamental concerns and the announcement of our decision to establish diplomatic relations was made on December 15.

We have been able to establish full diplomatic relations with the People's Republic of China in a way that protects the well-being of the people on Taiwan. The importance of this is fully reflected in the arrangements that we have been and will be establishing.

First, the United States will not abrogate the Mutual Defense Treaty. Rather, we have given notice that we will exercise our right to terminate the Treaty with Taiwan in accordance with its provisions, which permits termination by either party after one year's notice. All other treaties and agreements will remain in effect.

Second, is the critical question of the peaceful settlement of the Taiwan question by the Chinese themselves. It is clear from the actions and statements of the PRC in the last month that normalization has, in fact, enhanced the possibilities that whatever the ultimate resolution of the issue may be, it will be pursued by peaceful means.

Since the normalization of relations, the PRC has adopted a markedly more moderate tone on the Taiwan issue:

—On January 9 of this year, Vice Premier Deng told Senators Nunn, Glenn, Hart and Cohen, that, "The social system on Taiwan will be decided by the people of Taiwan. Changes might take 100 years or 1,000 years. By which I mean a long time. We will not change the society by force."

—On New Year's Day, after 25 years, the PRC ceasing firing propaganda artillery shells at the offshore islands of Quemoy and Matsu.

Third and finally, after the termination of the Mutual Defense Treaty on December 31, 1979, we will continue our previous policy of selling carefully selected defensive weapons to Taiwan. While the PRC said they disapproved of this, they nevertheless moved forward with normalization with full knowledge of our intentions.

In constructing a new relationship with the people on Taiwan, we are taking practical steps to ensure continuity of trade, cultural, and other unofficial relations. The President has taken steps to assure the uninterrupted continuation of such relations from January 1, 1979. In the future these relations will be conducted through a nonprofit nongovernmental corporation called the American Institute in Taiwan. This corporation will facilitate ongoing, and we are confident, expanding ties between the American people and the people on Taiwan. Taipei will handle its unofficial relations with this country in similar fashion.

Let me say a word or two about the American Institute in Taiwan, the legislation it requires, and its operations. Congress will be asked to approve an omnibus bill that will authorize the funding of the American Institute in Taiwan and confirm its authority to act in a wide range of areas. I hope we will have your active support for expeditious passage of the bill.

The Institute will have its headquarters in Washington with field offices in Taiwan. It will provide the full range of commercial and other services that have been previously provided through official channels to businessmen, both from the United States and from

Taiwan. In your private business dealings on Taiwan, you may freely contact the Institute's staff for advice or can deal directly with local firms and the authorities there. In short, we see no change necessary in the way private American business has been conducted on Taiwan up to now. EXIM loans, OPIC guarantees and other important arrangements will continue.

With these new arrangements in place, we expect Taiwan to continue to prosper. Taiwan's dynamic economic growth is one of the most impressive stories of the last decade; it is now our eighth largest trading partner, and per capita income is among the highest in Asia.

As anyone who has studied the issue can attest, normalization of relations with Peking was not an easy step to take. The difficulties always argued for themselves, and further delay was always an inviting option for any President. But we all recognized that sooner or later we would have to move. As I have already said, failure to try to move forward would have left us in danger of moving backwards—at great cost to our global position. By the time we took the decisive step every other member of NATO, our two treaty partners in ANZUS, and Japan had long since recognized the PRC, as had most other nations of the world. They were ready for our action—and most of them, including all the members of the Association of Southeast Asian Nations, applauded it.

When we acted, we did so in a way that enhances significantly the prospects for stability and peace in Asia and the Pacific. We acted in a way that will move us toward our objective of a stable system of independent nations in Asia, and that will also increase the chances of maintaining a stable equilibrium among the United States, Japan, China, and the Soviet Union.

The United States will continue to play an active role in order to maintain that stable equilibrium. For reasons of geography, history and economics, we are as much a Pacific nation as an Atlantic nation, with deep and abiding national interests in the region. We will maintain balanced and flexible military forces in the region, as the recent, successful conclusion of the base agreements with the Philippines so clearly demonstrates. And we will not hesitate to act, as required, to protect our vital national interests.

The rapidly expanding relations between our two nations in science, trade and exchanges require the kind of structure that diplomatic relations can provide. It will allow a much freer exchange between our cultures. And with full relations, we are in a far better position to encourage China's role as a constructive member of the world community. We will be discussing all of these matters with Vice Premier Deng when he visits us in two weeks.

It is particularly useful on this occasion to note some of the economic benefits we expect to flow from the establishment of diplomatic relations with the PRC. These include our participation as a regular supplier of agricultural commodities to China, the ability of U.S. exporters to compete on an equal basis with other suppliers, and the resumption of shipping, air, banking, and other normal economic relations with China.

Let me emphasize that in normalizing relations we acted in a way that does not threaten any other nation, but can increase the sense of community of nations that we seek to encourage.

We believe that China has an important role to play in the search for global peace and stability. The same is true for the Soviet Union. Our national interests are best served when we seek to improve realtions with both nations while protecting our vital strategic interests. This was the case during the late winter and spring of 1972, a period during which both the Shanghai Communique and SALT I were achieved. Equilibrium and stability, not isolation, are our strategic objectives. For this reason, we also look forward to the early conclusion of the SALT agreement with the Soviet Union and to improvement of our trade relations with the Soviets as well as the Chinese.

In conclusion, let me urge you to support the President's decision and the legislation to continue relations with the people on Taiwan. We seek your support in explaining the strategic and historic necessity of this action. And we encourage you to develop greater trade and contact with both the people on the mainland and Taiwan.

It was just short of seven years from the Shanghai Communique to normalization of relations. Through a difficult period, two great nations began to restore contact and shape a new relationship. We all recognize that a new era is upon us. Opportunities previously denied to us have now begun to take shape.

The nations grouped in and around the world's largest ocean, the Pacific, contain close to half the world's population. These nations must decide whether to choose the path of greater cooperation and growth or to enter into a period of unresolved struggles for influence.

For our part, the United States will enter the closing decades of the 20th century ready to play a leading role in the search for peace and economic well-being. The lack of diplomatic relations between the United States and China was an obstacle to progress for many years. Having now surmounted it, we face the tremendous challenge ahead with a sense of excitement and hope.

148

Appendix 8

"Relations With the People on Taiwan," Memorandum for All Departments and Agencies, December 30, 1978, 44 Fed. Reg. 1075 (1979)

As President of the United States, I have constitutional responsibility for the conduct of the foreign relations of the nation. The United States has announced that on January 1, 1979, it is recognizing the government of the People's Republic of China as the sole legal government of China and is terminating diplomatic relations with the Republic of China. The United States has also stated that, in the future, the American people will maintain commercial, cultural and other relations with the people of Taiwan without official government representation and without diplomatic relations. I am issuing this memorandum to facilitate maintaining those relations pending the enactment of legislation on the subject.

I therefore declare and direct that:

(A) Departments and agencies currently having authority to conduct or carry out programs, transactions, or other relations with or relating to Taiwan are directed to conduct and carry out those programs, transactions, and relations beginning January 1, 1979, in accordance with such authority and, as appropriate, through the instrumentality referred to in paragraph D below.

(B) Existing international agreements and arrangements in force between the United States and Taiwan shall continue in force and shall be performed and enforced by departments and agencies beginning January 1, 1979, in accordance with their terms and, as appropriate, through that instrumentality.

(C) In order to effectuate all of the provisions of this memorandum, whenever any law, regulation, or order of the United States refers to a foreign country, nation, state, government, or similar entity, departments and agencies shall construe those terms and apply those laws, regulations, or orders to include Taiwan.

(D) In conducting and carrying out programs, transactions, and other relations with the people on Taiwan, interests of the people of the United States will be represented as appropriate by an unofficial instrumentality in corporate form, to be identified shortly.

(E) The above directives shall apply to and be carried out by all departments and agencies, except as I may otherwise determine.

I shall submit to the Congress a request for legislation relative to nongovernmental relationships between the American people and the people on Taiwan.

This memorandum shall be published in the FEDERAL REGISTER.

JIMMY CARTER

Appendix 9

Taiwan Relations Act of 1979, Pub. L. No. 96-8, 93 Stat. 14 (codified at 22 U.S.C. §§ 3301-3316 (Supp. III 1979))

An Act

To help maintain peace, security, and stability in the Western Pacific and to promote the foreign policy of the United States by authorizing the continuation of commercial, cultural, and other relations between the people of the United States and the people on Taiwan, and for other purposes.

Be it enacted by the Senate and House of Representatives of the United States of America in Congress assembled,

SHORT TITLE

SECTION 1. This Act may be cited as the "Taiwan Relations Act".

FINDINGS AND DECLARATION OF POLICY

SEC. 2. (a) The President having terminated governmental relations between the United States and the governing authorities on Taiwan recognized by the United States as the Republic of China prior to January 1, 1979, the Congress finds that the enactment of this Act is necessary—

(1) to help maintain peace, security, and stability in the Western Pacific; and

(2) to promote the foreign policy of the United States by authorizing the continuation of commercial, cultural, and other

relations between the people of the United States and the people on Taiwan.

(b) It is the policy of the United States—

(1) to preserve and promote extensive, close, and friendly commercial, cultural, and other relations between the people of the United States and the people on Taiwan, as well as the people on the China mainland and all other peoples of the Western Pacific area;

(2) to declare that peace and stability in the area are in the political, security, and economic interests of the United States, and are matters of international concern;

(3) to make clear that the United States decision to establish diplomatic relations with the People's Republic of China rests upon the expectation that the future of Taiwan will be determined by peaceful means;

(4) to consider any effort to determine the future of Taiwan by other than peaceful means, including by boycotts or embargoes, a threat to the peace and security of the Western Pacific area and of grave concern to the United States;

(5) to provide Taiwan with arms of a defensive character; and

(6) to maintain the capacity of the United States to resist any resort to force or other forms of coercion that would jeopardize the security, or the social or economic system, of the people on Taiwan.

(c) Nothing contained in this Act shall contravene the interest of the United States in human rights, especially with respect to the human rights of all the approximately eighteen million inhabitants of Taiwan. The preservation and enhancement of the human rights of all the people on Taiwan are hereby reaffirmed as objectives of the United States.

IMPLEMENTATION OF UNITED STATES POLICY WITH REGARD TO TAIWAN

SEC. 3. (a) In furtherance of the policy set forth in section 2 of this Act, the United States will make available to Taiwan such defense articles and defense services in such quantity as may be necessary to enable Taiwan to maintain a sufficient self-defense capability.

(b) The President and the Congress shall determine the nature and quantity of such defense articles and services based solely upon their judgment of the needs of Taiwan, in accordance with procedures established by law. Such determination of Taiwan's defense needs shall include review by United States military authorities in connection with recommendations to the President and the Congress.

(c) The President is directed to inform the Congress promptly of any threat to the security or the social or economic system of the people on Taiwan and any danger to the interests of the United States arising therefrom. The President and the Congress shall determine, in accordance with constitutional processes, appropriate action by the United States in response to any such danger.

APPLICATION OF LAWS: INTERNATIONAL AGREEMENTS

SEC. 4. (a) The absence of diplomatic relations or recognition shall not affect the application of the laws of the United States with respect to Taiwan, and the laws of the United States shall apply with respect to Taiwan in the manner that the laws of the United States applied with respect to Taiwan prior to January 1, 1979.

(b) The application of subsection (a) of this section shall include, but shall not be limited to, the following:

(1) Whenever the laws of the United States refer or relate to foreign countries, nations, states, governments, or similar entities, such terms shall include and such laws shall apply with respect to Taiwan.

(2) Whenever authorized by or pursuant to the laws of the United States to conduct or carry out programs, transactions, or other relations with respect to foreign countries, nations, states, governments, or similar entities, the President or any agency of the United States Government is authorized to conduct and carry out, in accordance with section 6 of this Act, such programs, transactions, and other relations with respect to Taiwan (including, but not limited to, the performance of services for the United States through contracts with commercial entities on Taiwan), in accordance with the applicable laws of the United States.

(3)(A) The absence of diplomatic relations and recognition with respect to Taiwan shall not abrogate, infringe, modify, deny, or otherwise affect in any way any rights or obligations (including but not limited to those involving contracts, debts, or property interests of any kind) under the laws of the United States heretofore or hereafter acquired by or with respect to Taiwan.

(B) For all purposes under the laws of the United States, including actions in any court in the United States, recognition of the People's Republic of China shall not affect in any way the ownership of or other rights or interests in properties, tangible and intangible, and other things of value, owned or held on or prior to December 31, 1978, or thereafter acquired or earned by the governing authorities on Taiwan.

(4) Whenever the application of the laws of the United States depends upon the law that is or was applicable on Taiwan or compliance therewith, the law applied by the people on Taiwan shall be considered the applicable law for that purpose.

(5) Nothing in this Act, nor the facts of the President's action in extending diplomatic recognition to the People's Republic of China, the absence of diplomatic relations between the people on Taiwan and the United States, or the lack of recognition by the United States, and attendant circumstances thereto, shall be construed in any administrative or judicial proceeding as a basis for any United States Government agency, commission, or department to make a finding of fact or determination of law, under the Atomic Energy Act of 1954 and the Nuclear Non-Proliferation Act of 1978, to deny an export license application or to revoke an existing export license for nuclear exports to Taiwan.

(6) For purposes of the Immigration and Nationality Act, Taiwan may be treated in the manner specified in the first sentence of section 202(b) of that Act.

(7) The capacity of Taiwan to sue and be sued in courts in the United States, in accordance with the laws of the United States, shall not be abrogated, infringed, modified, denied, or otherwise affected in any way by the absence of diplomatic relations or recognition.

(8) No requirement, whether expressed or implied, under the laws of the United States with respect to maintenance of diplomatic relations or recognition shall be applicable with respect to Taiwan.

(c) For all purposes, including actions in any court in the United States, the Congress approves the continuation in force of all treaties and other international agreements, including multilateral conventions, entered into by the United States and the governing authorities on Taiwan recognized by the United States as the Republic of China prior to January 1, 1979, and in force between them on December 31, 1978, unless and until terminated in accordance with law.

(d) Nothing in this Act may be construed as a basis for supporting the exclusion or expulsion of Taiwan from continued membership in any international financial institution or any other international organization.

OVERSEAS PRIVATE INVESTMENT CORPORATION

SEC. 5. (a) During the three-year period beginning on the date of enactment of this Act, the $1,000 per capita income restriction in clause (2) of the second undesignated paragraph of section 231 of the Foreign Assistance Act of 1961 shall not restrict the activities of the Overseas Private Investment Corporation in determining whether to provide any insurance, reinsurance, loans, or guaranties with respect to investment projects on Taiwan.

(b) Except as provided in subsection (a) of this section, in issuing insurance, reinsurance, loans, or guaranties with respect to investment projects on Taiwan, the Overseas Private Insurance Corporation shall apply the same criteria as those applicable in other parts of the world.

THE AMERICAN INSTITUTE OF TAIWAN

SEC. 6. (a) Programs, transactions, and other relations conducted or carried out by the President or any agency of the United States Government with respect to Taiwan shall, in the manner and to the extent directed by the President, be conducted and carried out by or through—

(1) The American Institute in Taiwan, a nonprofit corporation incorporated under the laws of the District of Columbia, or

(2) such comparable successor nongovernmental entity as the President may designate,

(hereafter in this Act referred to as the "Institute").

(b) Whenever the President or any agency of the United States Government is authorized or required by or pursuant to the laws of the United States to enter into, perform, enforce, or have in force an agreement or transaction relative to Taiwan, such agreement or transaction shall be entered into, performed, and enforced, in the manner and to the extent directed by the President, by or through the Institute.

(c) To the extent that any law, rule, regulation, or ordinance of the District of Columbia, or of any State or political subdivision thereof in which the Institute is incorporated or doing business, impedes or otherwise interferes with the performance of the functions of the Institute pursuant to this Act, such law, rule, regulation, or ordinance shall be deemed to be preempted by this Act.

SERVICES BY THE INSTITUTE TO UNITED STATES CITIZENS ON TAIWAN

SEC. 7. (a) The Institute may authorize any of its employees on Taiwan—

(1) to administer to or take from any person an oath, affirmation, affidavit, or deposition, and to perform any notarial act which any notary public is required or authorized by law to perform within the United States;

(2) to act as provisional conservator of the personal estates of deceased United States citizens; and

(3) to assist and protect the interests of United States persons by performing other acts such as are authorized to be performed outside the United States for consular purposes by such laws of the United States as the President may specify.

(b) Acts performed by authorized employees of the Institute under this section shall be valid, and of like force and effect within the United States, as if performed by any other person authorized under the laws of the United States to perform such acts.

TAX EXEMPT STATUS OF THE INSTITUTE

SEC. 8. (a) The Institute, its property, and its income are exempt from all taxation now or hereafter imposed by the United States (except to the extent that section 11(a)(3) of this Act requires the imposition of taxes imposed under chapter 21 of the Internal Revenue Code of 1954, relating to the Federal Insurance Contributions Act) or by any State or local taxing authority of the United States.

(b) For purposes of the Internal Revenue Code of 1954, the Institute shall be treated as an organization described in sections 170(b)(1)(A), 170(c), 2055(a), 2106(a)(2)(A), 2522(a), and 2522(b).

FURNISHING PROPERTY AND SERVICES TO AND OBTAINING SERVICES FROM THE INSTITUTE

SEC. 9. (a) Any agency of the United States Government is authorized to sell, loan, or lease property (including interests therein) to, and to perform administrative and technical support functions and services for the operations of, the Institute upon such terms and conditions as the President may direct. Reimbursements to agencies under this subsection shall be credited to the current applicable appropriation of the agency concerned.

(b) Any agency of the United States Government is authorized to acquire and accept services from the Institute upon such terms and conditions as the President may direct. Whenever the President determines it to be in furtherance of the purposes of this Act, the procurement of services by such agencies from the Institute may be effected without regard to such laws of the United States normally applicable to the acquisition of services by such agencies as the President may specify by Executive order.

(c) Any agency of the United States Government making funds available to the Institute in accordance with this Act shall make arrangements with the Institute for the Comptroller General of the United States to have access to the books and records of the Institute and the opportunity to audit the operations of the Institute.

TAIWAN INSTRUMENTALITY

SEC. 10. (a) Whenever the President or any agency of the United States Government is authorized or required by or pursuant to the laws of the United States to render or provide to or to receive or accept from Taiwan, any performance, communication, assurance, undertaking, or other action, such action shall, in the manner and to the extent directed by the President, be rendered or provided to, or received or accepted from, an instrumentality established by Taiwan which the President determines has the necessary authority under the laws applied by the people on Taiwan to provide assurances and take other actions on behalf of Taiwan in accordance with this Act.

(b) The President is requested to extend to the instrumentality established by Taiwan the same number of offices and complement of personnel as were previously operated in the United States by the governing authorities on Taiwan recognized as the Republic of China prior to January 1, 1979.

(c) Upon the granting by Taiwan of comparable privileges and immunities with respect to the Institute and its appropriate personnel, the President is authorized to extend with respect to the Taiwan instrumentality and its appropriate personnel, such privileges and immunities (subject to appropriate conditions and obligations) as may be necessary for the effective performance of their functions.

SEPARATION OF GOVERNMENT PERSONNEL FOR EMPLOYMENT WITH THE INSTITUTE

SEC. 11. (a)(1) Under such terms and conditions as the President may direct, any agency of the United States Government may separate from Government service for a specified period any officer or employee of that agency who accepts employment with the Institute.

(2) An officer or employee separated by an agency under paragraph (1) of this subsection for employment with the Institute shall be entitled upon termination of such employment to reemployment or reinstatement with such agency (or a successor agency) in an appropriate position with the attendant rights, privileges, and benefits which the officer or employee would have had or acquired had he or she not been so separated, subject to such time period and other conditions as the President may prescribe.

(3) An officer or employee entitled to reemployment or reinstatement rights under paragraph (2) of this subsection shall, while continuously employed by the Institute with no break in continuity of service, continue to participate in any benefit program in which such officer or employee was participating prior to employment by the Institute, including programs for compensation for job-related death, injury, or illness; programs for health and life insurance; programs for annual, sick, and other statutory leave; and programs for retirement under any system established by the laws of the United States; except that employment with the Institute shall be the basis for participation in such programs only to the extent that employee deductions and employer contributions, as required, in payment for such participation for the period of employment with the Institute, are currently deposited in the program's or system's fund or depository. Death or retirement of any such officer or employee during approved service with the Institute and prior to reemployment or reinstatement shall be considered a death in or retirement from Government service for purposes of any employee or survivor benefits acquired by reason of service with an agency of the United States Government.

(4) Any officer or employee of an agency of the United States Government who entered into service with the Institute on approved leave of absence without pay prior to the enactment of this Act shall receive the benefits of this section for the period of such service.

(b) Any agency of the United States Government employing alien personnel on Taiwan may transfer such personnel, with accrued allowances, benefits, and rights, to the Institute without a break in service for purposes of retirement and other benefits, including continued participation in any system established by the laws of the United States for the retirement of employees in which the alien was participating prior to the transfer to the Institute, except that employment with the Institute shall be creditable for retirement purposes only to the extent that employee deductions and employer

contributions, as required, in payment for such participation for the
period of employment with the Institute, are currently deposited in
the system's fund or depository.

(c) Employees of the Institute shall not be employees of the United
States and, in representing the Institute, shall be exempt from
section 207 of title 18, United States Code.

(d)(1) For purposes of sections 911 and 913 of the Internal Revenue
Code of 1954, amounts paid by the Institute to its employees shall not
be treated as earned income. Amounts received by employees of the
Institute shall not be included in gross income, and shall be exempt
from taxation, to the extent that they are equivalent to amounts
received by civilian officers and employees of the Government of the
United States as allowances and benefits which are exempt from
taxation under section 912 of such Code.

(2) Except to the extent required by subsection (a)(3) of this
section, service performed in the employ of the Institute shall not
constitute employment for purposes of chapter 21 of such Code and
title II of the Social Security Act.

REPORTING REQUIREMENT

SEC. 12. (a) The Secretary of State shall transmit to the Congress
the text of any agreement to which the Institute is a party. However,
any such agreement the immediate public disclosure of which would,
in the opinion of the President, be prejudicial to the national security
of the United States shall not be so transmitted to the Congress but
shall be transmitted to the Committee on Foreign Relations of the
Senate and the Committee on Foreign Affairs of the House of
Representatives under an appropriate injunction of secrecy to be
removed only upon due notice from the President.

(b) For purposes of subsection (a), the term "agreement"
includes—

(1) any agreement entered into between the Institute and the
governing authorities on Taiwan or the instrumentality established by Taiwan; and

(2) any agreement entered into between the Institute and an
agency of the United States Government.

(c) Agreements and transactions made or to be made by or through
the Institute shall be subject to the same congressional notification,
review, and approval requirements and procedures as if such agreements and transactions were made by or through the agency of the
United States Government on behalf of which the Institute is acting.

(d) During the two-year period beginning on the effective date of this Act, the Secretary of State shall transmit to the Speaker of the House of Representatives and the Committee on Foreign Relations of the Senate, every six months, a report describing and reviewing economic relations between the United States and Taiwan, noting any interference with normal commercial relations.

RULES AND REGULATIONS

SEC. 13. The President is authorized to prescribe such rules and regulations as he may deem appropriate to carry out the purposes of this Act. During the three-year period beginning on the effective date of this Act, such rules and regulations shall be transmitted promptly to the Speaker of the House of Representatives and to the Committee on Foreign Relations of the Senate. Such action shall not, however, relieve the Institute of the responsibilities placed upon it by this Act.

CONGRESSIONAL OVERSIGHT

SEC. 14. (a) The Committee on Foreign Affairs of the House of Representatives, the Committee on Foreign Relations of the Senate, and other appropriate committees of the Congress shall monitor—

(1) the implementation of the provisions of this Act;

(2) the operation and procedures of the Institute;

(3) the legal and technical aspects of the continuing relationship between the United States and Taiwan; and

(4) the implementation of the policies of the United States concerning security and cooperation in East Asia.

(b) Such committees shall report, as appropriate, to their respective Houses on the results of their monitoring.

DEFINITIONS

SEC. 15. For purposes of this Act—

(1) the term "laws of the United States" includes any statute, rule, regulation, ordinance, order, or judicial rule of decision of the United States or any political subdivision thereof; and

(2) the term "Taiwan" includes, as the context may require, the islands of Taiwan and the Pescadores, the people on those islands, corporations and other entities and associations created or organized under the laws applied on those islands, and the governing authorities on Taiwan recognized by the United States as the Republic of

China prior to January 1, 1979, and any successor governing authorities (including political subdivisions, agencies, and instrumentalities thereof).

AUTHORIZATION OF APPROPRIATIONS

SEC. 16. In addition to funds otherwise available to carry out the provisions of this Act, there are authorized to be appropriated to the Secretary of State for the fiscal year 1980 such funds as may be necessary to carry out such provisions. Such funds are authorized to remain available until expended.

SEVERABILITY OF PROVISIONS

SEC. 17. If any provision of this Act or the application thereof to any person or circumstance is held invalid, the remainder of the Act and the application of such provision to any other person or circumstance shall not be affected thereby.

EFFECTIVE DATE

SEC. 18. This Act shall be effective as of January 1, 1979.

Approved April 10, 1979.

Appendix 10

Chairman Hua Gives Press Conference, Peking Review, no. 51, pp. 9-11 (Dec. 22, 1979)

Hua Kuo-feng, Chairman of the Central Committee of the Communist Party of China and Premier of the State Council, gave a press conference in Peking's Great Hall of the People on the morning of December 16 in connection with the establishment of diplomatic relations between the People's Republic of China and the United States of America.

Chairman Hua started the press conference by reading out the joint communique on the establishment of diplomatic relations between China and the United States and the statement of the Government of the People's Republic of China. He then answered questions from newsmen.

Question: Chairman Hua, will you please speak about the significance of the normalization of Sino-U.S. relations?

Answer: The normalization of Sino-U.S. relations has long been a wish of the Chinese and American peoples. Our great leader the late Chairman Mao Tsetung and our esteemed Premier Chou En-lai paved the way for opening Sino-U.S. relations. During the visit of President Nixon and Dr. Kissinger to China in 1972, the Chinese and U.S. sides issued the Shanghai Communique, which started the process of normalizing Sino-U.S. relations. Thanks to the joint efforts of the leaders, governments and peoples of the two countries in the past few years, Sino-U.S. relations have now been normalized. Former U.S. President Ford, many of the senators and congressmen and other friends from all walks of life have all played their part towards this end. Now, President Carter, Dr. Brzezinski and Secretary of State Vance have all made valuable contributions to the eventual normalization of our relations.

The establishment of diplomatic relations between China and the United States is a historic event. It opens up broad vistas for enhancing understanding and friendship between the two peoples and promoting bilateral exchanges in all fields. It will also contribute to peace and stability in Asia and the world as a whole. The Chinese and American peoples are happy about it and I believe the people all over the world will be happy at the news too.

Q: Chairman Hua, my question is: What policy will the Chinese Government adopt towards Taiwan in the new circumstances when relations between China and the United States have been normalized?

A: Taiwan is part of China's sacred territory and the people in Taiwan are our kith and kin. It is the common aspiration of all the Chinese people including our compatriots in Taiwan to accomplish the great cause of reunifying the country with Taiwan returning to the embrace of the motherland. It has been our consistent policy that all patriots belong to one big family whether they come forward early or late. We hope that our compatriots in Taiwan will join all the other Chinese people including our compatriots in Hongkong and Macao and overseas Chinese in making further contributions to the cause of reunifying China.

Q: Can you say that after normalization China would object to a visit to Taiwan by an American official?

A: The relations between China and the United States have been normalized after the joint efforts of both sides which have reached an agreement and have now issued the joint communique. And the answer to your question is clearly stated in the joint communique which I quote: "The United States of America recognizes the Government of the People's Republic of China as the sole legal Government of China. Within this context, the people of the United States will maintain cultural, commercial, and other unofficial relations with the people of Taiwan." So the answer is very clear in this paragraph. There will only be unofficial relations.

Q: Will the United States be permitted to continue providing Taiwan with access to military equipment for defensive purposes?

A: Paragraph two of the joint communique which I announced just now says: "The United States of America recognizes the

Government of the People's Republic of China as the sole legal Government of China. Within this context, the people of the United States will maintain cultural, commercial, and other unofficial relations with the people of Taiwan.'' In our discussions on the question of the commercial relations, the two sides had differing views. During the negotiations the U.S. side mentioned that after normalization it would continue to sell limited amount of arms to Taiwan for defensive purposes. We made it clear that we absolutely would not agree to this. In all discussions the Chinese side repeatedly made clear its position on this question. We held that after the normalization continued sales of arms to Taiwan by the United States would not conform to the principles of the normalization, would be detrimental to the peaceful liberation of Taiwan and would exercise an unfavourable influence on the peace and stability of the Asia-Pacific region. So our two sides had differences on this point. Nevertheless, we reached an agreement on the joint communique.

Q: Mr. Chairman, may I ask you please about the possibility of a worsening of relations with Russia as a result of what you have announced today, since the Russians may be very suspicious of your joining more closely with the Americans. Do you feel that it may lead to a worsening of relations with Moscow?

A: We think that the normalization of relations between China and the United States and the signing of the Treaty of Peace and Friendship Between China and Japan are conducive to peace and stability in the Asia-Pacific region and the world as a whole. Does this mean the formation of an axis or alliance of China, Japan and the United States? We say that it is neither an alliance nor an axis. China and the United States have now normalized their relations and the relations between the United States and the Soviet Union have also been normalized. Therefore it is out of the question that the normalization of relations is directed at any country.

Here I would like to make an additional explanation. China has now normalized relations with the United States and Japan and signed a treaty of peace and friendship with Japan. This is beneficial to the development of relations between countries in the Asia-Pacific region and to the peace and stability of the Asia-Pacific region and the world as a whole. Undoubtedly, of course, it is also favourable to the struggle of all peoples against hegemonism. We have mentioned our opposition to hegemonism in our joint communique. We oppose both big hegemony and small hegemony, both global hegemony and regional hegemony. This will be conducive to the peace of the whole world.

Q: I would like to ask you if there were any Chinese compatriots from Taiwan involved at any stage in the discussions towards normalization?

A: No.

Huang Hua, Chinese Foreign Minister, and Chang Wen-chin, Vice-Foreign Minister, attended the press conference. More than 100 Chinese and foreign correspondents were present.

Appendix 11

Message to Compatriots in Taiwan, Beijing Review, no. 1, pp. 16-7 (Jan. 5, 1979).

The Standing Committee of the Fifth National People's Congress at its Fifth Plenary Session on December 26, 1978 adopted after discussion a message to compatriots in Taiwan. Following is the full text of the message.—Ed.

Dear Compatriots in Taiwan:

Today is New Year's Day 1979. We hereby extend our cordial and sincere greetings to you on behalf of the people of all nationalities on the mainland of our motherland.

As an old saying goes, "When festival times come round people think all the more of their loved ones." On this happy occasion as we celebrate New Year's Day, our thoughts turn all the more to our kith and kin, our old folks, our brothers and sisters, in Taiwan. We know you have the motherland and your kinsfolk on the mainland in mind too. This mutual feeling of many years standing grows with each passing day. From the day when Taiwan was unfortunately separated from the motherland in 1949, we have not been able to communicate with or visit each other, our motherland has not been able to achieve reunification, relatives have been unable to get together, and our nation, country and people have suffered greatly as a result. All Chinese compatriots and people of Chinese descent throughout the world look forward to an early end to this regrettable state of affairs.

The Chinese nation is a great nation. It accounts for almost a quarter of the world's population and has a long history and brilliant culture, and its outstanding contributions to world civilization and human progress are universally recognized. Taiwan has been an inalienable part of China since ancient times. The Chinese nation has great vitality and cohesion. Throughout its history, foreign invasions and internal strife have failed to split our nation permanently. Taiwan's separation from the motherland for nearly 30 years has been artificial and against our national interests and aspirations, and this state of affairs must not be allowed to continue. Every Chinese, in Taiwan or on the mainland, has a compelling responsibility for the survival, growth and prosperity of the Chinese nation. The important task of reunifying our motherland, on which hinges the future of the whole nation, now lies before us all; it is an issue no one can evade or should try to. If we do not quickly set about ending this disunity so that our motherland is reunified at an early date, how can we answer our ancestors and explain to our descendants? This sentiment is shared by all. Who among the descendants of the Yellow Emperor wishes to go down in history as a traitor?

Radical changes have taken place in China's status in the world over the past 30 years. Our country's international prestige is rising constantly and its international role becomes ever more important. The people and governments of almost all countries place tremendous hopes on us in the struggle against hegemonism and in safeguarding peace and stability in Asia and the world as a whole. Every Chinese is proud to see the growing strength and prosperity of our motherland. If we can end the present disunity and join forces soon, there will be no end to our contributions to the future of mankind. Early reunification of our motherland is not only the common desire of all the people of China, including our compatriots in Taiwan, but the common wish of all peace-loving peoples and countries the world over.

Reunification of China today is consonant with popular sentiment and the general trend of development. The world in general recognizes only one China, with the Government of the People's Republic of China as its sole legal Government. The recent conclusion of the China-Japan Treaty of Peace and Friendship and the normalization of relations between China and the United States show still more clearly that no one can stop this trend. The present situation in the motherland, one of stability and unity, is better than ever. The people of all nationalities on the mainland are working hard with one will for the great goal of the four modernizations. It is our fervent hope that Taiwan returns to the embrace of the motherland at an early date so that we can work together for the great cause of national development. Our state leaders have firmly declared that they will take present realities into account in accomplishing the great cause of reunifying the motherland and respect the status quo on Taiwan and the opinions of people in all walks of life there and adopt reasonable policies and measures in settling the question of reunification so as not to cause the people of Taiwan any losses. On the other hand, people in all walks of life in Taiwan have expressed their yearning for their homeland and old friends, stated their desire "to identify themselves with and rejoin their kinsmen," and raised diverse proposals which are expressions of their earnest hope for an early return to the embrace of the motherland. As all conditions now are favourable for reunification and everything is set, no one should go against the will of the nation and against the trend of history.

We place hopes on the 17 million people on Taiwan and also the Taiwan authorities. The Taiwan authorities have always taken a firm stand of one China and have been opposed to an independent Taiwan. We have this stand in common and it is the basis for our co-operation. Our position has always been that all patriots belong to one family. The responsibility for reunifying the motherland rests with each of us. We hope the Taiwan authorities will treasure national interests and make valuable contributions to the reunification of the motherland.

The Chinese Government has ordered the People's Liberation Army to stop the bombardment of Jinmen (Quemoy) and other islands as from today. A state of military confrontation between the two sides still exists along the Taiwan Straits. This can only breed man-made tension. We hold that first of all this military confrontation should be ended through discussion between the Government of the People's Republic of China and the Taiwan authorities so as to create the necessary prerequisites and a secure environment for the two sides to make contacts and exchanges in whatever area.

The prolonged separation has led to inadequate mutual understanding between the compatriots on the mainland and on Taiwan and various inconveniences for both sides. Since overseas Chinese residing in faraway foreign lands can return for visits and tours and hold reunions with their families, why can't compatriots living so near, on the mainland and on Taiwan, visit each other freely? We hold that there is no reason for such barriers to remain. We hope that at an early date transportation and postal services between both sides will be established to make it easier for compatriots of both sides to have direct contact, write to each other, visit relatives and friends, exchange tours and visits and carry out academic, cultural, sports and technological interchanges.

Economically speaking, Taiwan and the mainland of the motherland were originally one entity. Unfortunately, economic ties have been suspended for many years. Construction is going ahead vigorously on the motherland and it is our wish that Taiwan also grows economically more prosperous. There is every reason for us to develop trade between us, each making up what the other lacks, and carry out economic exchanges. This is mutually required and will benefit both parties without doing any harm to either.

Dear compatriots in Taiwan,

The bright future of our great motherland belongs to us and to you. The reunification of the motherland is the sacred mission history has handed to our generation. Times are moving ahead and the situation is developing. The earlier we fulfill this mission, the sooner we can jointly write an unprecedented, brilliant page in the history for our country, catch up with advanced powers and work together with them for world peace, prosperity and progress. Let us join hands and work together for this glorious goal!

Appendix 12

Statement of ROC Foreign Minister Yen-shih Tsiang at the ROC-U.S. Talks on Postnormalization Relations, Dec. 28, 1978, News From China, Dec. 29, 1978, at 78-1344

The Republic of China has been a long-standing ally of the United States of America. The government and people of the Republic of China have persistently cooperated with the United States in maintaining world peace and upholding the principles of justice. On December 16 [Taipei time], however, President Carter abruptly announced his decision to sever diplomatic relations with our country, to serve notice of his intention to recognize the Chinese Communist regime as of January 1, 1979, and to terminate the Sino-American Mutual Defense Treaty.

I do not consider that the U.S. government has any justifiable cause at all to unilaterally announce its intention to terminate the defense treaty which, as you know, is a treaty of alliance. In addition, so long as the defense treaty between our countries continues to remain in full force and effect, I cannot understand how President Carter can take the position that the diplomatic relations between our two countries can be terminated before that treaty of alliance comes to an end.

We strongly oppose this decision which we believe is wrong, and which has most seriously impaired the rights and interests of this country. We are convinced that it will also impair the long-term interests of the United States and endanger the peace and stability of the Asian-Pacific region. Although President Carter's decision is so far-reaching, we were advised of it only seven hours before it was made public. This is not the way for a leading world power to treat a long-standing ally and it has aroused indignation among the Chinese people both at home and abroad. President Chiang Ching-kuo has made a solemn statement on our position on this unfortunate event. I will not repeat it, but I do hereby lodge a further protest on behalf of my government against the decision of President Carter.

I will now state the fundamental position of my government as the basis of the talks between our two governments.

First, since the founding of the Republic of China in 1911, she has maintained close and friendly relations with the United States. The people of the United States fought shoulder to shoulder with our people during the Second World War.

The close cooperation with the United States continued after the seat of our government moved to Taipei, with the United States government providing us with military and economic aid to help us build our armed forces and expedite our economic development. We have now become your country's eighth trading partner and our total volume of trade with your country has outstripped that of the Chinese Communist regime by nearly ten times. Today we have economic and cultural relations with more than 140 countries and territories. We also maintain diplomatic ties with more than twenty countries.

The Republic of China continues to be an independent sovereign state with an efficient government supported by her people. She has consistently made positive contributions to security, stability and peace in the West Pacific. The U.S. government must recognize these realities.

Second, President Carter has repeatedly expressed his concern for the security and well-being of the people of the Republic of China. This concern must be backed with assurance of security for this region. To build such an assurance merely on the judgment and expectation that the Chinese Communists would not invade Taiwan by the use of force is unrealistic, dangerous, and would have serious consequences. Therefore, the United States must provide concrete and specific measures, through appropriate legislation, to ensure the security of the Republic of China, including the uninterrupted supply of weapons which we need now and in the future.

Finally, I must point out that there are now some 59 treaties and agreements, as well as other arrangements between our two countries. Furthermore, additional agreements and other government-to-government arrangements will be required from time to time to meet future needs. Appropriate legislative measures, therefore, must be taken by your government to ensure that existing treaties, agreements and arrangements continue to remain in full force and effect; and new ones be entered into between our two countries. All these, I emphasize, are essential to the maintenance of future ties between our two countries.

Appendix 13

President Chiang Ching-Kuo's Five Principles on U.S.-ROC Relations, Summary by Dr. James Chu-yul Soong, Deputy-Director of the Government Information Office, of President Chiang Ching-kuo's statement to Deputy Secretary of State Warren Christopher at the U.S.-ROC post-normalization discussions, News From China, Dec. 29, 1978, at 78-1348

The Republic of China is an independent sovereign state with a legitimately established government based on the Constitution of the Republic of China. It is an effective government, which has the wholehearted support of her people. The international status and personality of the Republic of China cannot be changed merely because of the recognition of the Chinese Communist regime by any country of the world. The legal status and international personality of the Republic of China is a simple reality which the United States must recognize and respect.

The United States has expressed its intention that it will continue to maintain cultural, economic, trade, scientific, technological, and travel relations with the Republic of China. The ties that bound our two countries and people together in the past, however, include much more than these. The Republic of China is ready and willing to continue these traditional ties. The United States, on the other hand, must also realize the importance of the continuity of these ties, not only in their present scope, but also on an expanded scale to meet future needs.

The security of the Asian-Pacific region is also of utmost importance to the well-being and livelihood of the 17 million people on Taiwan, as well as American interests in the area.

The Sino-U.S. Mutual Defense Treaty signed in 1954 was designed to be a vital link in the chain of collective defense system of free countries in the West Pacific. The situation in this region has not changed. It is still unstable and insecure. The threat of invasion and subversion by Communist forces to the free nations of Asia, particularly after the fall of Vietnam, is even more serious than before.

Hence, the U.S. unilateral action to terminate the Sino-U.S. Mutual Defense Treaty will further destabilize this region and might create a new crisis of war. Thus, in order to ensure the peace and security of the West Pacific, which includes that of the Republic of China, it is imperative that the United States take concrete and effective measures to renew its assurances to countries in this region.

We are ready and determined to continue to do our share in securing stability and peace in the West Pacific. But in order to do this, we must have sufficient capabilities to defend ourselves, and thereby protect our neighbors. President Carter has indicated that he is still concerned about the peace, security, and prosperity of this region after the termination of the Sino-U.S. Mutual Defense Treaty, and will continue to supply the Republic of China with defense weapons. The U.S. must give us assurances of a legal nature which would ensure the fulfillment of this commitment.

We are at present faced with the pragmatic problems involved in continuing and maintaining 59 treaties and agreements, as well as other arrangements, between our two countries. Since both the Republic of China and the United States are governed by law, the private interests of both Chinese and American citizens require the protection of definite legal provisions. Appropriate legislative measures in both countries must therefore be taken to provide legal basis on which these security, commercial, and cultural treaties and agreements can continue to remain in full force and effect.

The complex nature of the activities of mutual interest to our two countries makes it impossible for them to be carried out by any private organization or individual. To facilitate the continuation and expansion of all relations between our two countries, it is necessary that government-to-government level mechanisms be set up in Taipei and Washington. This model alone can serve as the framework on which the future relationship of our two countries can be constructed.

Appendix 14

Declaration of Formosans (1964). By P'eng Ming-min in collaboration with Hsieh Ts'ung-min and Wei T'ing-ch'ao. Translated and issued by United Formosans in America for Independence

A powerful movverment is rapidly developing inside Formosa. It is a self-preservation movement of the island's 12 million people who are willing neither to be ruled by the Chinese Communists nor to be destroyed by the Chinese Nationalist regime. Riding high the universal current of awakening peoples, we dedicate ourselves to the overthrow of the Government of Chiang Kai-shek and to the establishment of a free, democratic and prosperous society. We believe it to be the privilege as well as the responsibility of every one of us to take part in this great movement and help realize our supreme goal at the earliest possible date.

I

That there are one China and one Formosa is an iron fact. In Europe or in America, in Africa or in Asia, whether or not one has already accorded diplomatic recognition to the Chinese Communist Government, the entire world accepts the fact of one China and one Formosa.

Even in the U.S. which finds herself isolated from the rest of the world in her Asian policy, there is only a small number of reactionary politicians who toy with the idea of "non-recognition." The mainstream of American public opinion, particularly that of intellectuals, demands *de jure* recognition of one China and one Formosa as the final solution for the Chinese question. America's foreign policy is evolving toward that direction. Why then does the U.S. continue to support the Chiang regime, at least verbally, as the sole and legitimate Government of China? It is because the U.S. wants to use this (recognition of the Chiang regime) in her diplomatic bargaining with Communist China so that a compromise favorable to her may be attained. The U.S. has conferred with Communist China over a hundred times in Warsaw. Throughout the meetings she has emphasized that if only Communist China relinquishes her demand to "liberate" Taiwan, America's door will forever remain open to China.

The Chiang regime depends on the Seventh Fleet for its survival. We must not be blinded by the myth of the "Return to the Mainland" and be led down the path of destruction. Once the Seventh Fleet is withdrawn the collapse of the Chiang regime is just a matter of a few hours. Indeed, "Return to the Mainland" is merely a pretext whereby Chiang maintains his illegal regime and suppresses the people.

II

"Return to the Mainland" is not even remotely possible! Any person with a minimum of common sense will come to such a conclusion without a moment's hesitation. The troops under Chiang's control are, at best, a defensive force; they cannot be an adequate offensive force. Their existence depends entirely on American military aid and the aim of American aid is to maintain America's defense perimeter in the Pacific. For this reason Chiang's troops cannot obtain any weapons beyond the need for defense. Chiang's navy has no ability to wage warfare independently because it has neither battleships nor adequate shipyard facilities. Chiang's airforce is composed chiefly of short-range fighters. The number of transport planes and long-range fighters which are indispensable to launching an offensive is so miserably small. Chiang's army, as always, has only a lightly equipped infantry for its main force. Mechanized troops and heavy artillery are only for window dressing.

Formosa is economically unable to support a counterattack. Even though Chiang may try to support his troops with every means available, including military expenditures which amount to over 80% of the national budget, it is much too great a burden for such a small island to support several hundred thousand troops even in peace time, let alone war time. And what about the human resources needed to replace casualties?

Thus the reason for war no longer can be justified. Nonetheless, while preaching freedom and democracy Chiang Kai-shek violates basic human rights at will, monopolizes political power and through the use of secret police imposes a dictatorial rule. Some people say the Chinese mainlanders are eager to return to their homeland and therefore readily accept Chiang Kai-shek's enslavement. The truth of the matter, however, is that the growing prestige of Communist China has given pride to the nationalistic Chinese who feel that their country has for the past 100 years been subjected to foreign humiliation. They are convinced that the corrupt and inefficient Chiang Kai-shek regime could not possibly have made China what she is today. For whom then are we to fight? For what are we to fight? Who is foolish enough to sacrifice his life for Chiang Kai-shek now that the dictator has failed to present the people with convincing reasons for war?

Chiang Kai-shek's officers and soldiers have devoted their entire lives to their master. But what has been their reward? Once they grow old they are retired with no guarantee of financial security and are cast into the civilian population only to roam the streets for their living. This kind of situation naturally creates bitterness among retired soldiers. Their resentment is best expressed in the often heard sarcasm: "Just as it was the retired soldiers who toppled the Chiang regime on the mainland, so will they again topple it in Formosa."

Life for the active officers and soldiers is even worse. They often complain: "Mao Tze-tung has severed us from our ancestors, but Chiang Kai-shek has severed us from our descendants." Some who are daring risk their lives; others who are less daring let their resentment smolder. More and more officers and soldiers violate military regulations. Commanders seek to appease their soldiers instead of disciplining them. As a result soldiers become more arrogant than their officers. The morale of the troops is exceedingly low.

As for those Formosan youth drafted into the Nationalist army to replace the retired Chinese soldiers the dreadful memory of the February 28 Incident in which 20,000 Formosan leaders were massacred by Chiang Kai-shek still lingers. Daring not to speak out, they nevertheless remain Chiang Kai-shek's "silent enemy." Dressed in military uniforms, they reveal no evidence of their inner thoughts. It is not difficult to assume, however, that under no circumstances will they acknowledge "a thief as their father" and accept Chiang Kai-shek's enslavement.

The system of political commissars interferes in the performance of the military and reduces its efficiency. The characteristic of any military activity lies in the accomplishment of its mission through quick movement of manpower and material. The system of political commissars on the other hand, emphasizes political doctrine and surveillance of military personnel. Under the system the political aim is emphasized more than the military aim and political responsibilities restrict military efficiency. Many an enlightened officer in the Nationalist army such as General Sun Li-jen protested the system, but he was falsely accused of harboring Communists and to this day has not been acquitted. Both officers and soldiers say: "If the order for mobilization should come we want first to execute the political commissars."

Imagine an army with no ability to wage offensive warfare, with no economic resources to support war operations, with soldiers' morale flagging, with low military efficiency and with no justifiable objectives of war trying to confront a powerful army of Chinese Communists. This war is called "Return to the Mainland." Thus the stubborn 5-star General Chiang Kai-shek can be compared with Don Quixote comically raising his worn-out broom challenging a windmill to a fight.

III

Why then is Chiang Kai-shek so persistent in demanding the "Return"? Because this slogan is the only means by which he prolongs his political power and enslaves the people. For 15 years, using this empty slogan like a bad check which is bound to bounce later, he has justified the enforcement of martial law and held 12 million people under tight military control. Indeed, his scheme of "Return to the Mainland" is the greatest act of deception of the 20th century.

Needless to say, Kuomintang officials themselves realize that such deception cannot last much longer. On the one hand they send abroad their children and the wealth which they have plundered from the people, in full preparation for emergency escape. On the other hand they act like "doctors" keeping alive their dying, obstinate patient, Chiang Kai-shek, by giving him the life-prolonging drug of "Return to the Mainland."

Let us examine what magic power this slogan has yielded:

First, by taking advantage of the psychological weakness of the people, it has prolonged the life of the Chiang regime which would otherwise have lost its *raison d'etre*. Some Chinese mainlanders are very homesick and have supported Chiang Kai-shek out of the illusion

that they may one day return to their homeland. Even some Formosans have been led to believe in the slogan because of their hope that
Chiang's return to the mainland would remove from them political
pressure and lighten the economic burden.

Secondly, in the name of national emergency it has been used as
a pretext to suspend normal enforcement of the constitution and other
laws, to persecute those who out of patriotism and a sense of justice
criticize the regime, and to enforce such repressive policies as control
of speech, thought and censorship of press.

Thirdly, by insisting to attack Red China, the Chiang regime has
enhanced its position in diplomatic bargaining with the U.S. It has
been used as a tool to extort more aid from the U.S. When negotiations between the U.S. and China are stalled or when the U.S. applies
too much pressure on Chiang, he immediately releases the rumor in
Hong Kong that negotiations for peace between Peking and Taipei
are in the making, thus confusing the U.S. who has been suffering
from acute neurosis over Red China.

In summary, the slogan of "Return to the Mainland" enhances
the position of the Chiang regime externally by proposing to attack
Red China and enables it internally to enforce dictatorial rule and
prolong the regime's life.

IV

Whom does the Chiang Kai-shek regime represent?

The Nationalist regime claims to be "China's sole and legitimate
government." It insists that the representatives of the National
Assembly, members of the Legislative and Control Yuans are all
elected from the people. They include representatives of both the
Chinese mainland and Formosa. We all know, however, that elections
for those representatives were held 18 years ago (1947). We also
know that in less than 2 years (1949) the Chinese people on the
mainland had disowned the Chiang regime because of its corruption
and inefficiency. Chiang was quickly kicked out of the Chinese
mainland in spite of the fact that he commanded millions of soldiers.
Clearly the people on the mainland had already selected their own
government. If the Nationalist Government could not represent the
people of the mainland of that time, how can it claim to represent a
new generation of people 18 years later? Clearly Chiang cannot
represent the people on the mainland today.

Can the Chiang regime represent the people of Formosa? Out of
some 3000 representatives of the National Assembly the Formosan

representatives occupy only 10 or so seats. Out of 473 members of the
Legislative Yuan only 6 are Formosans. Their terms expired 12 and 15
years ago respectively. They certainly have no right to represent
Formosans today. What is more, in the February 28 Incident Chiang
massacred 20,000 leading Formosans (at that time Formosa only had
a population of 6 million). Although Formosans have not since raised
their voice they remain always Chiang Kai-shek's "silent enemy."

Speaking of Formosans and mainlanders, we must point out that
when the Chiang regime proposes that the two groups must cooperate, it does not really mean it. On the contrary, it is very much afraid
of cooperation between the two groups and has, in fact, employed
every means available to divide them. This policy can most clearly be
observed in the elections. The Chiang regime wants to make sure that
Formosans and mainlanders are divided and made mutually suspicious and independent from one another so that they can be manipulated and controlled. Therefore, the Chiang regime has deliberately
prevented Formosans and liberal mainlanders from cooperating in
their attempt to overthrow Chiang's dictatorship and establish a true
democracy. When Lei Chen sought to unify Formosans and mainlanders, Chiang finally removed his disguise and imprisoned the liberal
magazine editor after falsely accusing him of being Communist in
outright disregard of protests both at home and abroad. Chiang
Kai-shek knows clearly that the day Formosans and mainlanders
achieve cooperation will be the day his government will collapse.

Some argue that the Chiang regime represents the Kuomintang;
and since the Party and State are traditionally one, it, therefore,
represents China. In truth, however, the Chiang regime cannot even
represent the Kuomintang. The Kuomintang itself is a symbol of
dictatorship. There is no democracy whatsoever. Its members have
no freedom of speech. In their conventions their representatives can
only listen to their leader, nodding, bowing and applauding. They are
simply a group of yes-men capable only of approving the proposals
presented by their leader. They neither want nor dare to attempt to
question the content of proposals. Moreover within the Party there
are many factions. In their struggle for power the so-called Lian-
kwang faction (from the provinces of Kwangtung and Kwang-si) as
represented by Hu Han-min, Chang Fa-kuei, Li Tsung-jen, etc. has
already been liquidated. Other factions which have not been able to
gain the personal confidence of Chiang are not permitted to be a part
of the nucleus of the Party. Needless to say, those members who are
excluded from power are resentful of Chiang's leadership. The clever

members either resort to silent protest by not expressing any of their opinions or actively agitate their followers to form the mainstream of anti-Chiang forces within the Party.

We can only conclude that the Chiang regime is composed of a small minority of the Kuomintang. It cannot represent China, much less Formosa, and not even the Kuomintang itself.

V

Formosa's economic development is hampered by two grave problems: a huge military budget and a rapidly increasing population. They are the traps of self-destruction created by the irresponsible Chiang regime under the false slogan of "Return to the Mainland."

According to Chiang's statistics issued this year (1964), military expenditures account for more than 80% of the national budget. This amount does not include every military expense. Two hundred thousand tons of rice provided annually by the Food Bureau for the military are priced far below the market value and even below the official value set by the Bureau. Expenses for transportation, electricity and other services provided for the military by publically operated enterprises are never revealed. Income from military industry and from the resale of American aid and commodities go to the military. Thus, actual military expenditures is far in excess of the island's capital formation.

The rapidly increasing population also has the effect of hindering the growth of the economy. Its chief effect is unemployment, which grows worse every day, particularly in the villages. Formosa's labor population is estimated at 4,000,000 of which at least 1,000,000 are unemployed—one-fourth of the entire labor population. Every square kilometer of arable land is crowded with an average of 1,230 persons. Year after year thousands of elite youth graduated from colleges and universities are forced to go abroad. The Chiang regime is afraid to face this reality and seeks its solution in the self-deceiving scheme of the "Return to the Mainland." Even though some intellectuals give warning to the seriousness of the problem, it is all to no avail. Those who advocate birth control are labeled defeatist. Instead the Chiang regime encourages the population growth and pins its hope on the newborn babies, expecting that 20 years later their generation will take up arms and fight back to the mainland.

Many people believe that the land reform in Formosa has been the result of the virtuous policy of the Chiang Government. The truth is, however, that the purpose of the land reform is to weaken or even eliminate the potential strength of its opposition. Since the days of the Manchu dynasty, Formosa's political leaders traditionally came from the landowner class. Chiang Kai-shek is keenly aware that the rise of local leadership is detrimental to the success of his dictatorial rule. For this reason he first eliminated 20,000 Formosan leaders during the February 28 Incident of 1947 and then in 1950 enforced the so-called land reform policy aiming at overthrowing the traditional political leadership class. The fact that the Chinese mainlanders themselves are not landowners is another reason why the land reform policy was so smoothly carried out. As a result of Chiang's steadfast effort to eliminate the landowner class the local strength was greatly reduced. On the other hand, the farmers are suffering under artificially deflated farm prices, are not able to escape from exorbitant taxes, and are exploited due to the unfair ratio of exchange between crops and fertilizer. They spend every day working for a living, leaving no energy for other activities.

Any economic policy should have a consistent long-range development plan. Yet what the Chiang regime has made is a blind investment in total disregard of fundamental economic principles. Its aim is superficial and temporary, designed to meet a one-time need. In order to maintain military food allotments they even resort to the plundering of farmers, just as foolishly as one would kill a chicken to obtain an egg. They are afraid that any attempt to reform the present taxation system will result in a temporary suspension of their military budget; so instead of admitting the need for reform, they let it continue to deteriorate. In order to consolidate their power they collaborate with the rich and oppress the poor masses, thus creating an extremely insecure society where rich and poor are poles apart.

Let us take a look at the final phase of the Chiang regime which has been pushed into a desperate corner. On the one hand Chiang places his henchmen in various important posts to tighten his dictatorial rule. On the other he uses public bonds of NT$ 1.2 billion, derived from the enforcement of the urban real estate reform policy and from the sale of public enterprises and several times has sent his number one economic henchman, Hsu Po-yuan, to Central and South America for wholesale purchase of land.

VI

Can Formosa be an independent country?

A state is only an instrument through which people may pursue their happiness and prosperity. Any people who live under the same circumstances and share common interests may form a country. For more than 10 years Formosa has been an independent country in reality. On the basis of population, area, economic productivity and cultural standards, Formosa ranks about 30th among the more than 110 UN members. In fact, people of many small independent countries enjoy an even higher degree of social welfare and cultural advantage; for example, the Scandinavian countries, Switzerland and Uruguay in South America. We should stop imagining ourselves as a "big power" and instead face reality and establish a small but democratic and prosperous society.

Some people say that Chiang Kai-shek has become a "naked emperor"; therefore, we'll just wait until the day he passes away. But we must not overlook the possibility of a desperate Chiang regime handing Formosa over to Red China. Nor should we for even a moment forget that Formosa may become the victim of international power rivalries. We, therefore, must not just simply wait.

Many intellectuals are still obsessed by the idea of "peaceful transfer of government" and "progressive reform." We must point out that if we will review the history of the Kuomintang, we will at once discover that so long as an arrogant and despotic Chiang is alive any form of compromise with him is either an illusion or a deception designed especially to trap the intellectual appeasers. Therefore, we must not even dream of "peaceful transfer of government," and accept compromise.

We wish to take this opportunity to earnestly warn those who have been collaborating with the Chiang regime:

"You must immediately repent of your sins and pledge not to further collaborate with Chiang in oppressing the people of Formosa. Or else history will pass judgment on you and the people one day will make you pay the severest penalty possible."

VII

In a region such as Formosa which is still in the process of development, economic growth requires revolutionary changes in social, economic and political aspects. Among them politics is the fountainhead of power that generates changes. Although Formosa has a good foundation for modernization, we are still far from such a goal so long as the corrupt and inefficient Chiang regime exists. Consequently, we must not depend on the so-called "progressive reform."

Having recognized this fact, we set forth the following proposals and express our firm determination to fight for the realization of them even to the last drop of our blood:

A. Our Objectives:

1. To affirm that the "Return to the Mainland" is absolutely impossible and by unifying the strength of 12 million people, regardless of their place of birth, to overthrow the Chiang regime and establish a new country and a new government;

2. To adopt a new constitution which will guarantee basic human rights, and to establish an efficient government responsible to a congress which will enforce true democracy; and

3. To participate in the UN as a member of the Free World, and to establish diplomatic relations with other peace loving countries and together strive for world peace.

B. Our Principles:

1. To respect the principle of democracy and through a general election elect the head of state who should not be an idol to be worshiped nor should he be vested with absolute power immune from criticism, who as a public servant should dedicate himself to the people under the supervision and control of the congress:

2. To guarantee freedom of assembly, freedom of organization and freedom of expression and to enforce a system of political parties by granting an opposition party a legal position;

3. To eliminate special privileges, purge corruption and graft, tighten administrative discipline and improve the treatment of soldiers, teachers and public employees;

4. To establish a healthy civilian control of the government, enforce scientific supervision of the government, raise efficiency of administration and enforce clean and just politics;

5. To guarantee the independence of the judiciary, abolish laws which encroach upon basic human rights and forbid illegal arrest, interrogation and punishment;

6. To abolish the secret police system, and regulate the positions and functions of police officers according to the principles accepted by democratic countries, and to cultivate among the people a law-abiding spirit;

7. To guarantee the people's right to freely communicate both at home and abroad and to guarantee freedom of movement and travel and to maintain an open society; and

8. To reduce armament to the basic necessity of self-defense and guarantee the position and livelihood of retired soldiers.

In the field of economy, because military expenses will have been greatly reduced, we should be able to accelerate the development of the economy by fully utilizing manpower as well as material resources in accordance with a long-range plan. We shall by democratic means distribute our economic gains and abolish exclusive privileges enjoyed by any individual or class and guarantee equal economic opportunity. We shall establish a system of direct taxation, adopt a progressive income tax and an inheritance tax and eliminate the gap between rich and poor. We shall plan to increase the national productivity, reduce unemployment and raise the living standard of the people. In this way can the respect of mankind and the freedom of individuals be said to have true meaning.

We shall improve the traditional method of agricultural production, strive for the economic self-sufficiency of villages and establish a scientific, mechanized and modernized agricultural society. In the past the Chiang regime has blindly invested its capital, interfered in the operation of economic enterprise, supported the capitalists by supplying low-wage laborers, deprived the farmers of their harvest through the so-called fertilizer-crop exchange program and enormously increased the burden of the public through the increase of indirect taxes; e.g., sales and household taxes. For those problems created by Chiang's economic maladministration we shall seek fundamental solutions.

We are convinced that the purpose of our society is to maintain the dignity of individuals and promote the welfare of the people. We are, therefore, opposed to any policy of terror, exploitation and such other measures aimed at hindering the unity of the people and the normal development of society. We shall dedicate ourselves to establishment of a benevolent society where people can trust and help each other and each individual may pursue a life which will bring him the greatest happiness.

VIII

For many a year the Chinese people have been given two extreme ways of judging values: the Kuomintang way of judgment on the extreme right and the Communist way of judgment on the extreme left. They have never been given an opportunity to exercise judgment on the basis of truth. We must free ourselves from the yoke of these two extremes. Even more urgently we must abandon the psychology of trying to solve our future by depending on either of the two extreme regimes. Outside the Kuomintang and the Communist

Party we must seek the third alternative of self-preservation in Formosa.

Let us put an end to those days of darkness! Let us call upon all those people unwilling to be ruled by Communists or to be destroyed by Chiang Kai-shek to unite in the struggle to overthrow Chiang's dictatorial regime and establish our own free country.

Dear compatriots who love democracy and freedom, let us not be discouraged and abandon our hope just because what we see today is dark. Conditions both at home and abroad are turning steadily in our favor. The strength of our movement is rapidly expanding. Our men have already penetrated inside the government, various local organizations, the armed forces, commercial enterprises, newspaper companies, schools, factories and villages. Our organization has already established close contact with our compatriots in the U.S., Japan, Canada, France and West Germany and has obtained their enthusiastic support. Once the time is ripe our men will appear at every corner of the land and together with you they shall fight for freedom.

Dear compatriots, victory is already in sight. Let us rise and be united!

This declaration is the symbol of our struggle. From today on it will appear before you wherever you are or may go. Remember, while you are reading it, our organization is continuing to expand and our movement is powerfully developing.

Please circulate.

Please reproduce.

Please quote.

Appendix 15

A Declaration on Human Rights by the Presbyterian Church in Taiwan, August 16, 1977

To the President of the United States, to all countries concerned, and to Christian Churches throughout the world:

Our church confesses that Jesus Christ is Lord of all mankind and believes that human rights and a land in which each one of us has a stake are gifts bestowed by God. Therefore we make this declaration, set in the context of the present crisis threatening the 17 million people of Taiwan.

Ever since President Carter's inauguration as President of the United States he has consistently adopted "Human Rights" as a principle of his diplomacy. This is an epoch-making event in the history of foreign policy.

We therefore request President Carter to continue to uphold the principles of human rights while pursuing the "normalization of relationships with Communist China" and to insist on guaranteeing the security, independence and freedom of the people of Taiwan.

As we face the possibility of an invasion by Communist China we hold firmly to our faith and to the principles underlying the United Nations Declaration of Human Rights. We insist that the future of Taiwan shall be determined by the 17 million people who live there. We appeal to the countries concerned—especially to the people and the government of the United States of America—and to Christian churches throughout the world to take effective steps to support our cause.

In order to achieve our goal of independence and freedom for the
people of Taiwan in this critical international situation, we urge our
government to face reality and to take effective measures whereby
Taiwan may become a new and independent country.

We beseech God that Taiwan and all the rest of the world may
become a place where "Mercy and truth will meet together; righteousness and peace will embrace. Truth shall spring out of the earth;
and righteousness shall look down from heaven." (Psalm 85 verses
10 and 11) (Today's English Version and King James Version)

> Signed   H.E. Chao
> Moderator of the General Assembly
> (at present out of the country)
>
> H.K. Weng
> Deputy Moderator of the General Assembly
> (Acting in the absence of the Moderator)
>
> C. M. Kao
> General Secretary